COUNT BASIE

Alun Morgan

Selected discography
by Alun Morgan

Spellmount
TUNBRIDGE WELLS

Hippocrene Books
NEW YORK

First published in the UK in 1984 by
SPELLMOUNT LTD
12 Dene Way, Speldhurst,
Tunbridge Wells, Kent TN3 0NX
ISBN 0 946771 50 2 (UK)

Morgan, Alun
    Count Basie – (Jazz Masters)
    1. Basie, Count   2. Jazz musicians – United States – Biography
    I. Title   II. Series
    785.42'092'4   ML 419.B19

First published in the USA by
HIPPOCRENE BOOKS INC.
171 Madison Avenue,
New York, NY 10016

ISBN 0 87052 012 1 (USA)

Series editor: John Latimer Smith
Cover design: Peter Theodosiou

Printed & bound in Great Britain
by Anchor/Brendon Ltd, Tiptree, Essex

Contents

Acknowledgements

The Bibliography lists the sources of much of the material which appears in the book but I would like also to express my most grateful thanks to my friends Mike Doyle, Charles Fox, Peter Lowe and Steve Voce and a very special paean to Tony Shoppee who supplied me with so very much information painstakingly culled from *Down Beat* magazines dating back to 1940. Tony has given the word 'lexicographer' a new dimension.

For Irene

Chapter One

'Count Basie isn't just a man, or even just a band,' remarked singer Lena Horne one night at Birdland, 'he's a way of life'. Just as Duke Ellington enjoyed a number of parallel careers, so Count Basie succeeded in leading his band, playing the piano and, perhaps most important, creating an environment in which many young soloists developed into highly talented individuals. Basie referred to himself as a 'non-pianist' but he played the piano in a way which brought out the very best in all his fellow musicians. He also had the ability to spot talent and remember the comparative unknown years later when he needed to restock his band or replace a sideman. Above all he enjoyed working. 'It's not because of the public that he's on the job before we are most nights' once remarked guitarist Freddie Green. 'It's to hear the band for his own kicks. He'll never stop playing'. In fact he struggled on against a heart attack and a combination of debilitating illnesses until cancer finally cut him down. The end came on April 26, 1984 at his home in Hollywood, Florida.

The beginning was nearly 80 years earlier. William Basie was born in Red Bank, New Jersey, on August 21, 1904 and brought up as an only child. (A brother died young.) Bill's mother gave him his first piano tuition but it was across the Hudson River, in New York, that he picked up his most valuable lessons. He wanted to be a drummer at the outset but 'Sonny Greer cut me loose from that! He used to fill in on gigs and take over'. There were plenty of keyboard idols in New York at the time, the ragtime pianists such as James P. Johnson, Lucky Roberts and Willie 'The Lion' Smith but for Basie there was one man above all others. 'Fats Waller was my guy, right to the end' he told Charles Fox years later. And it was Waller who introduced him to the pipe organ. 'The first time I saw him, I had dropped into the old Lincoln Theatre in Harlem and heard a young fellow beating it out on the organ. From that time on, I was a daily customer, hanging on to his every note, sitting behind him all the time, fascinated by the ease with which his hands pounded the keys and his feet manipulated the pedals. He got used to seeing me, as though I were part of the show. One day, he asked me whether I played the organ. "No", I said, "but I'd give my right arm to learn". The next day he invited me to sit in the pit and start working the pedals. I sat on the floor, watching his feet, and using my hands to imitate them. Then I sat beside him and he taught me'. New York teemed with places of entertainment providing work for pianists; cabarets, saloons, theatres, dance halls and the like to say nothing of the regular 'rent parties' put on to help those less fortunate than their fellows. On a good night Basie would earn ten dollars at such a party which helped in the payment of his own rent.

Through his friendship with Fats, Basie took Waller's place in a touring show, Katie Crippin And Her Kids, which was touring the vaudeville circuit. As Nat Shapiro has explained, such vaudeville shows 'played everything from big houses in Chicago, St. Louis, Memphis and New Orleans to store-front and tent theatres in the most rural areas of the Deep South'. Most of the shows were handled by TOBA (Theatre Owners Booking Association), known to many as Toby Time or, more impolitely, Tough On Black Asses for TOBA handled Negro entertainers while the Keith Orpheum circuit was responsible for the rest. Basie travelled hundreds of miles on circuit with shows such as 'Hippity Hop'. He also worked with blues singers such as Clara Smith and Maggie Jones and also played in trumpeter June Clark's band in a Fourteenth Street dance hall. Around 1925 he joined a road show presided over by Gonzelle White and stayed for the best part of two years until an event occured which, though innocuous in itself, was to have a lasting effect on his subsequent career. 'I'd travelled west from New York with a touring vaudeville show' he recalled later. 'I was just a kinda honky-tonk piano player with the show and we had more than our share of troubles. We didn't have any 'names' in the cast and we didn't do much business. So about the time we reached Kansas City, the unit was in pretty bad shape and then came the inevitable folding. When we folded, I was broke and didn't have any way to get out of town'.

He took a job playing piano in a silent cinema called the Eblon Theatre. The house director was James Scott, a leading ragtime composer and performer in the previous decade. It was Scott who wrote *Grace and beauty, Climax rag* and *Frog legs rag* but it seems very doubtful that Basie had any musical connexion with Scott during the period when, as he remarked later, he played for the better part of a year, 'all sorts of pictures, anything from a Western melodrama to a crime thriller or one of those passion plays'. Then in 1928 he joined Walter Page's Blue Devils. According to Jimmy Rushing, Basie had first heard the Blue Devils a year before when the Gonzelle White show was still in being. 'Basie was playing piano in the four-piece band and even acting the part of a villain in one of the comedy skits. It was on a Saturday afternoon and both bands were "ballyhoolin" from horse-drawn wagons. The Blue

1 The Count, publicity still, late 1930s (Melody Maker)

Devils were trying to entice customers to the Southern Barbecue, an open-air beer garden and Basie's band was advertising the White show. We were playing a piece called *Blue Devil blues* and up comes Basie and sits himself down at the piano. Man, but he played!' The precise chronology of those early days in Kansas City is difficult to determine not only because of the passage of time but also because of the hectic life lived by so many KC residents at the time. Years later Basie was still enthusing over his early days in Kansas City and referred to it as a 'wide-open city. That's where life began! You could do anything, go anywhere!' Others have described Kansas City in similar terms during what became known as the Pendergast Era. Tom Pendergast was the leader of the Democratic Party in Kansas City from 1927 until 1938, when he was eventually convicted on a charge of income-tax evasion. Pendergast encouraged gambling and all forms of night life. For a time he owned a 'wide-open' hotel, the Jefferson, and arranged for it to have police protection. Whatever one may think of Pendergast's dubious role as a leading light in KC, it is true to say that all the significant musical developments, including the formative work of Basie, Jay McShann, Charlie Parker etc., took place when Pendergast ran the city his way, with dozens of excellent bands playing at the many places of entertainment.

When Basie joined the Blue Devils the band was already rated very highly in the Southwest. Bill Basie joined a band which had Hot Lips Page, Buster Smith, Eddie Durham and Jimmy Rushing in its ranks. It was Walter Page's ambition to do battle with Kansas City's leading band of the day, Bennie Moten's orchestra. Frank Driggs has reported that 'Kansas City newspapers of the time indicate that Moten did battle with Page in 1928 at the Paseo Hall, and Page is said to have blown Moten out'. So fiercely partisan was the following for bands in those days that such a defeat could strongly affect business and it is said that Bennie Moten made an offer to take over the Blue Devils, keeping Walter Page as the leader but using Moten's name at the front. Page would not agree but after he had a run of bad luck with bookings, Moten was in a strong position to make offers to individual Blue Devils. He enticed Basie and Eddie Durham away in the early part of 1929 then, later that year, won over Rushing and Hot Lips Page. The Blue Devils broke up in 1931 when Walter Page himself joined Moten and the only factual evidence we have of what was claimed to be a band which was better than Moten's are two 78rpm sides, *Blue Devil blues* (with a vocal by Rushing and a trumpet solo from Lips Page) and *Squabblin'*, a riff composer-credited to Basie and with solos from the Count himself and Buster Smith. (The discographies list these two Vocalion sides as dating from November, 1929 but Jimmy Rushing's claim that they were made the previous year is more likely to be correct.)

Basie remembered that with Moten 'I guess we played just about every jazz spot in Kansas City. The ones that are foremost in my mind are the Reno Club, the Tower and Main Street Theatres, the Fairland Park and Pla-mor Ballrooms and the Frog Hop Ballroom in St. Joseph, not far from Kansas City'. With the infusion of talent from the Blue Devils, Moten's band began to take on a new character. It now had a five-man brass section, (bigger than that of any other KC band at the time) and the written arrangements by Eddie Durham and Basie demanded a higher standard of discipline within the brass and reed sections. During 1931 Bennie Moten took the band East on a tour, bought about 40 new arrangements from Benny Carter and Horace Henderson and at the end of the year effected more personnel changes. Walter Page (on bass now; the tuba had been rejected), Eddie Barefield, Ben Webster and, for a time, trumpeter Joe Smith came into the band. With Durham, Basie and Barefield all writing for the band and tunes such as *Moten swing* and *Toby* enriching the book, the Moten band achieved a sound which, judged from the recordings made for Victor in December, 1932, was the genesis of the later Count Basie orchestra.

But, as Frank Driggs has made clear in his essay 'Kansas City And The Southwest', these changes were not to the liking of the public who wanted Moten to go on serving up the mixture as before. They looked upon the smoother sound of the band as foreign to the tenets of Kansas City music and Moten suffered a humiliating defeat when he played at the annual Musicians' Ball at Paseo Hall where he was pitted against bands such as those led by Andy Kirk and Clarence Love. But it was a new band, the Kansas City Rockets led by ex-Moten trombonist Thamon Hayes, which wiped out Bennie. Morale in the Moten ranks was at a very low ebb and in 1934 Count Basie and a group of Bennie's men actually left to play under Count's leadership in Little Rock, Arkansas. (It is rumoured that both Buddy Tate and Lester Young were in this breakaway group.) But at that time Basie's name was not sufficient of a draw and Moten had no difficulty in coaxing the renegades back into his employ. By the end of 1934 Moten's brand of music was back in favour and although a booking at Chicago's Grand Terrace failed to materialise, the band went into the Rainbow Gardens in Denver, a prestigious locale for units in the 1930s. As Frank Driggs reports, 'Bennie himself stayed behind for a minor tonsillectomy. He was said to have had a cold at the time and he was unable to take ether, necessitating a local anaesthetic. He was a nervous person and had put off the operation for a long time, until it became necessary for his health; and he apparently moved at a crucial moment, so that the surgeon's scalpel severed his jugular vein. Bennie's surgeon was a prominent man in the Midwest, and he was forced to give up his practice and move to Chicago as a result of the accidental death. Irreparable damage was done to the morale of the men on the job in Denver, and they were unable to finish the engagement. Walter Page and 'Bus Moten each tried to rally the men and keep the band together, but it was no use; they disbanded for good in the summer of 1935'.

Basie did not 'take over' the Moten band on Bennie's death. Instead he formed a group of his own and succeeded in getting a booking at Kansas City's Reno Club, an establishment owned by 'Papa Sol' Epstein, one of Pendergast's men. The hours were incredibly long, often twelve hours at a stretch, and Count was paid twenty-one dollars a week with eighteen each for his sidemen. 'But we were all young then' said Basie years later 'and we couldn't wait to get to work. It was fun! And after work the guys went further up on 12th Street and jammed all morning'. He recalled the names of the men in that first Reno Club band when talking to Leonard Feather as 'three saxes, Buster Smith and another alto player, and Slim Freeman on tenor; three trumpets – Dee "Prince" Stewart, Joe Keyes and Carl (Tatti) Smith; plus Walter Page on tuba, myself, and the drummer Willie (Mac) Washington'. Hot Lips Page was also working at the Reno at the same time; he acted as Master of Ceremonies and sometimes sat in with the Basie brass. Surprisingly the Reno had broadcasting facilities over a local Kansas City station, W9XBY, which was then carrying out experimental transmissions. Each Sunday night the Reno Club band went on the air and for those occasions, Jimmy Rushing sat in with Basie. Lester Young heard one of the broadcasts and, by all accounts, sent Count a telegram saying that the band sounded fine except for the tenor player. Basie took the hint and brought in Lester as a replacement for Slim Freeman. The Reno was not exactly an impressive establishment. The signs outside advertised domestic Scotch at ten cents, imported Scotch at fifteen cents and beer at five cents. Hot dogs were ten cents each and hamburgers fifteen. The girls lounging outside were tacitly advertising the services they could offer on the floor above the dance hall. Musicians came and went in a fairly casual manner. 'I don't mind saying that it was a mad scuffle with that band' recalled Count. 'In fact, we were in and out of the Reno Club for about a year before things even started to look up'. There is often little point in conjecture but it would be interesting to know what form Basie's career might have taken if one single event had not occured. Radio, the medium which had been instrumental in bringing Doctor Crippen to justice, was about to play its part in altering the course of jazz.

Chapter Two

Towards the end of 1935 Benny Goodman brought his orchestra to Chicago for a triumphal return booking at the Congress Hotel, triumphal in the sense that in between its two Congress bookings, it had made history at the Palomar Ballroom across in Los Angeles. Benny was the 'King Of Swing' and the nation wanted to see and hear this vital and alive band. On hand was John Hammond, then 24 years of age and a keen, enthusiastic jazz fan. But Hammond was more than that; he was a Vanderbilt on his mother's side and had 'dropped out' of Yale in 1931 in order to promote jazz. He wrote for the British 'Melody Maker' and had a contract to produce records for the British market. Despite his youth, Hammond was an influential figure in jazz circles. His friendship with Benny Goodman developed and the family relationship was completed in 1941 when Goodman married Hammond's sister Alice. But in the last week of November, 1935, when Benny's band was floating on the crest of a wave, John was out in the car park of the Congress hotel, sitting in his car which was fitted with a powerful radio. 'I had a twelve-tube Motorola with a large speaker, unlike any other car radio in those days' Hammond wrote in his autobiography. 'I spent so much time on the road that I wanted a superior instrument to keep me in touch with music around the country. It was one o'clock in the morning. The local stations had gone off the air and the only music I could find was at the top of the dial, 1550 kilocycles, where I picked up W9XBY, an experimental station in Kansas City. The nightly broadcast by the Count Basie band from the Reno Club was just beginning. I couldn't believe my ears'. After that first hearing, an event which Leonard Feather has called 'the most momentous chance audition in jazz history', Hammond tuned in to W9XBY whenever he could. So intrigued was he by the sound of the band that he went down to KC to hear the music for himself. On his first visit to the Reno the first thing he saw was 'the high bandstand, at the top of which sat Jo Jones surrounded by his drums. Basie sat at the left with Walter Page and his bass crowded as close to the piano as he could get. In the front line were Lester Young, Buster Smith on alto, and Jack Washington on baritone. Behind them were two trumpets, Oran 'Lips' Page and Joe Keyes, and the trombone, Dan Minor. Jimmy Rushing, the famous Mr. Five-By-Five, sang the blues, and Hattie Noel, as big as Rushing and dressed in a ridiculous pinafore, was the comedienne and a fairly good singer'. No recordings of broadcasts from the Reno Club have come to light but, from first-hand descriptions of the music and the very earliest known Basie recordings it is possible to make a judgement on how the band probably sounded. It made extensive use of riffs both behind soloists and as launching pads. The arrangements (perhaps routines would be a more accurate description) were sufficiently flexible to allow soloists to take extra choruses if it happened that the inspirational level was high. And Basie himself? John Hammond has noted that 'Basie had developed an extraordinary economy of style. With fewer notes he was saying all that Waller and Hines could say pianistically, using perfectly timed punctuation – a chord, even a single note – which could inspire a horn player to heights he had never reached before'. Although Hammond was writing of Count at the time of the W9XBY broadcasts his description could be applied to Basie at almost any period. At the same time it would be a mistake to assume that Count had lost the art of two-handed playing. Sandwiched in the middle of the 1957 Roulette recording of *Kid from Red Bank*, for example, there are a couple of choruses of stride piano which would do credit to any masters of the idiom.

Hammond's enthusiasm for the Basie band went further than writing about it in *Down Beat* magazine. He urged Dick Altschuler of the American Record Company to sign the band for his Brunswick label. Altschuler agreed but, by a clever piece of fast manipulation, Dave Kapp, brother to Jack Kapp, head of Decca, got to Count first. The contract Basie signed was for twenty-four 78rpm sides a year for three years with a payment of 750 dollars to Basie for each of the three years. There were to be be no royalty payments or, in fact, any further money for Basie. Hammond did his best to redress the situation on Count's behalf but the fact remains that Basie never received any further payments for the 61 tracks he made for Decca between January, 1937 and February, 1939. When one considers that, amongst those 61 titles, were the original versions of *One o'clock jump, Topsy, Sent for you yesterday, Jumpin' at the Woodside, Jive at five, Blue and sentimental* etc, the iniquity of the Decca move can be judged. On the brighter side, Hammond managed to get Willard Alexander of the powerful Music Corporation of America (MCA) so interested in the band that he signed Basie to an MCA contract. Alexander booked the band into the Grand Terrace Hotel in Chicago, up until then the stronghold of the Earl Hines and Fletcher Henderson bands. With so much potential activity in the

2 Count Basie, late 1930s (Melody Maker)

offing, Basie set about enlarging his band. Joe Glaser had signed Hot Lips Page to a separate contract, thinking Page had a bigger future than the Count. In his place Basie secured the services of Buck Clayton, who up to that time had not intended to stay in KC longer than a few days. (He was on his way east from California in order to join Willie Bryant's band.) 'I was with Basie two months at the Reno Club,' states Clayton. 'We left Kansas City October 31, 1936, Halloween Night, the same night we had played in a battle of bands with Duke Ellington at the Paseo Ballroom. In our minds, we thought we had won the battle, but when we got on the bus to leave there wasn't one single friend of ours on hand to assure us we had. So probably we didn't, and, knowing Duke as I know him now, I'm almost sure we didn't'.

If there was uncertainty about who won at the Paseo Ballroom there was no doubt about the Basie band's position when they opened at the Grand Terrace. 'They had us playing the *Poet and Peasant* Overture as our big show number' Basie recalled later. 'The band just didn't make it, and there was nothing in the show that gave us a real chance to display ourselves properly'. John Hammond was more forthright. 'Remembering those first nights at the Grand Terrace, I am astonished they were not fired. They struggled through Ed Fox's show arrangements, but the chorus girls loved the band because it was so easy to dance to. Jo Jones, a dancer himself, knew how to play for dancers. Fletcher Henderson came to the rescue, allowing Basie to use half his library of arrangements, one of the generous gestures which endeared Fletcher to so many musicians.' The Basie band played the Grand Terrace from November 7, 1936 to December 3, a period in which owner Ed Fox claimed the Terrace did its smallest business in years. (He tried to cancel the Basie booking but MCA ignored his plea; the agency was more interested in the radio wire which the club had.) But the Grand Terrace booking was probably Basie's first and greatest hurdle. Pitchforked into an entirely new musical environment was like being thrown in at the deep end. Years later Jimmy Rushing blamed the Count for some of the band's shortcomings. 'It was Basie who couldn't read, and the troubles started when Tiny Parham had written an arrangement for the band of the William Tell Overture. Basie couldn't play the piano part so we had to call in a woman who was a music teacher, and she took over the piano'. Away from the Grand Terrace a small group from the band achieved greatness. John Hammond, incensed at Decca's signing of the band to a recording contract, decided to record Basie for himself, albeit as part of a group under someone else's leadership. The date for the session is usually given as October 8 or 9 but the band was still in Kansas City at that time. Years later Hammond gave the date of November 9, 1936 which seems far more likely. The records came out on the Vocalion label under the name 'Jones – Smith Inc.' and they contain the first (and some would claim the best) examples of Lester Young on record. The full band used *Lady be good* and *Shoeshine boy* as part of its repertoire; these small group versions allow Young to spin out long melodic lines of a character which was entirely fresh to those brought up to believe that the sound of the tenor saxophone was epitomised by the work of Coleman Hawkins.

After the Grand Terrace booking came to an end, Basie moved East, playing a series of dates prior to his engagement at New York's Roseland Ballroom just before New Year's day. The band's spirits must have been at a low ebb after the Grand Terrace debacle and, as Hammond reports, a one-night stand at New London, Connecticut, on the way to New York did little for morale. 'They played (New London) on the night of a terrible New England storm' remembers Hammond, 'in a ballroom which normally held about sixteen hundred. That night there were no more than four hundred'. In an attempt to broaden the band's appeal, the musicians knocked together arrangements of popular songs and found that they were also expected to play tangos and rhumbas. 'Woody Herman was playing opposite us at the Roseland' said Basie. 'He was breaking in his band too, but he was *in* there – he had made it. We had a rough time at the Roseland, but the manager there stuck with us – he believed in what we wanted to do'. The New York booking also gave Decca the chance to record the band for the the first time, a unit which now boasted five brass (Buck Clayton, Tatti Smith and Joe Keyes on trumpets, George Hunt and Dan Minor on trombones), four saxes and four rhythm. Lead alto Buster Smith, suspicious of the MCA contract, had refused to leave Kansas City for the Chicago and New York engagements so Basie brought in Caughey Roberts, who had played in California with Buck Clayton. By now the band boasted two exceptional and contrasting tenors in Lester Young and the Texas-born Herschel Evans. Claude 'Fiddler' Williams doubled guitar and violin (although he played only the former on the record date) and the band was completed by Reno stalwarts Jo Jones, Walter Page and Jack Washington. Those first four titles, *Honesuckle Rose* (solos by Basie, Young and Tatti Smith), *Pennies from Heaven* (Rushing vocal), *Swinging at the Daisy Chain* (Basie, Buck Clayton, Herschel Evans, Walter Page and Jo Jones) and *Roseland*

Shuffle (solos from Basie and Lester Young) give a very clear indication of the band's enormous capabilities and unrivalled solo strength. At the Roseland Basie played before a segregated audience for the ballroom enforced its 'whites only' ruling so strictly that Puerto Ricans were discouraged. From the Roseland the band moved on to the Apollo Theatre on 125th Street. This Harlem entertainment centre had been a proving ground for talent since it first opened its doors in 1934 and Basie was apprehensive about the reception he could expect. Willard Alexander still had confidence in Basie's ability to succeed and he persuaded the Apollo management to spend extra money to promote the Count and his men. As John Hammond wrote later 'Nobody in Harlem will ever forget that opening. Basie passed the test. He was on his way'. But Alexander's next booking for the band cast them back in the melting pot for he moved them into the William Penn Hotel in Pittsburgh, the best hotel in the city which had never previously had a Negro band in residence. Fortunately for us an LP exists (Jazz Archives JA–16, 'The Count At The Chatterbox') recorded from the network radio broadcasts which were done from the hotel. One can now imagine the impact Basie's music must have had on the staid and sedate atmosphere. Hammond went to the opening and reported 'Bill did his best to accommodate the William Penn customers, muting the brass, keeping the guys on their best behaviour, but the band couldn't help swinging'. The 'Chatterbox' album is a valuable document for it is the earliest 'live' recording of the Basie band to appear. The music bursts with inner enthusiasm and although this was a thirteen-man ensemble it has the feel of a small group, so well-integrated are the backing riffs behind the soloists. The evidence is here that, by this date at least, Count had refined his own piano playing to the point where he only played the notes that mattered. The contrast between the full power of the band and Basie's relaxed keyboard figurations is a joy.

After the William Penn Hotel booking the band did a string of one-nighters gaining impetus at each date. The network radio broadcasts plus the first Decca releases, *Pennies from Heaven* coupled with *Swingin' at the Daisy Chain* and *Honeysuckle Rose* backed with *Roseland Shuffle*, all helped the band to establish its reputation. Lester Young and Herschel Evans now had their own groups of supporters at the various dance halls and Basie was not slow to feature the tenor 'battles'. This was the foundation for many similar musical wars of attrition in later years and for Basie's assertion that 'the band starts with the rhythm section then builds up to the tenors'. Jimmy Rushing sang the blues and the band was beginning to make some real money but MCA felt that it would be even more of a success with a girl singer on the pay roll. In March, 1937 Billie Holiday joined the band but, due to conflicting contracts, she was not allowed to make records with the Count. (Nevertheless she may be heard on a handful of titles which have appeared as parts of broadcast transcriptions dating from 1937.) Billie's stay with Basie lasted less than a year although she herself referred to it as 'almost two years' in her autobiography 'Lady Sings The Blues', a book which cannot be relied upon too much for factual matters. This was obviously an unhappy period for both Bill and Billie; Jimmy Rushing accused her of not acting in a professional way and Billie complained that the money she was paid did not cover her laundry bills and other expenses. Basie and Holiday parted company at the beginning of 1938 and Billie made no secret of the fact that she blamed John Hammond for her dismissal. Willard Alexander sprang to Hammond's defence; 'it was John Hammond who got Billie the job with Count Basie' he was reported as saying in *Down Beat*, 'and he was responsible for Basie keeping her. In fact, if it hadn't been for John Hammond, Billie would have been through six months sooner. The reason for her dismissal was strictly one of deportment, which was unsatisfactory, and a distinctly wrong attitude towards her work. Billie sang fine when she felt like it. We just couldn't count on her for consistent performance'. Hammond was soon at work behind the scenes on Basie's behalf. Having convinced Count already that Freddie Green would make a greater contribution to the rhythm section than Claude Williams, he was directing Basie's attention towards a singer who was both consistent and professional, Miss Helen Humes.

Chapter Three

The arrival of Helen Humes in July, 1938 was the last important addition to a band which had now become nationally famous. No longer could it be looked upon as a 'territory' unit which had tried to storm the bastion of the New York dance halls, scuttling back to Kansas City when it needed reassurance. Basie had made important changes to his personnel and with Helen and Rushing sharing the vocals the ensemble comprised Ed Lewis on lead trumpet with Buck Clayton and Harry Edison sharing the solos, trombonists Dan Minor, Benny Morton and Dicky Wells, Earl Warren on alto leading Herschel Evans and Lester Young on tenors and Jack Washington doubling baritone and alto plus the 'All American Rhythm Section' of Basie, Freddie Green, Walter Page and Jo Jones. Prior to Basie's bookings in New York the Duke Ellington, Cab Calloway and Chick Webb bands held sway with Benny Goodman coming on strongly. It was the era when bands tried to 'cut' each other and one such contest took place at the Savoy Ballroom on January 16, 1938, the night of Benny Goodman's Carnegie Hall concert at which Basie, Buck Clayton, Lester Young, Freddie Green and Walter Page had participated. *Metronome* magazine for February of that year reported 'Count Basie did it! For years, nobody was able to lick Chick Webb and his Chicks within the walls of his own Savoy Ballroom, but on January 16, notables such as Duke, Norvo, Bailey, Duchin, Krupa and Goodman heard the Count gain a decision over the famed Chick. It was a matter of solid swing to the heart triumphing over sensational blows to the head'. Years later, during the Seventies when Charles Fox interviewed Basie on the radio and suggested that Webb had come second that night Count was vehement in his denial. 'Absolutely not! There was no cutting! We played together and we were lucky to get out with just a few bruises!' This is consistent with Basie's self-effacement and his outspoken admiration for men such as Webb, Duke Ellington and Oscar Peterson. But the fact remained that Basie's band was now a potent force in the hierarchy. Count based himself at New York's Woodside Hotel and held court in the basement, auditioning new arrangements from outsiders such as Don Redman, Jimmy Mundy and Andy Gibson. The turning point was the band's summer booking into the tiny 'Famous Door' club at 66 West 52nd Street. 'The band first started clicking at the Famous Door' recalls Buck Clayton. 'We had made good changes and the band sounded well together. The place was small and we sat close together, and the low ceilings made the band sound beautiful, and it was a rocking place, and that's where business started picking up'. The Famous Door was the second 52nd Street premises to bear the name; it measured 20 to 25 feet wide and 50 to 60 feet deep. Frank Driggs, who contributed a valuable sleeve note to Jazz Archives JA–41 'Count Basie At The Famous Door 1938–1939' states that when the Columbia Broadcasting System did its regular broadcasts from the club, 'the patrons had to remove themselves to the sidewalk in order to achieve clear transmission from the cramped, mirrored club'. Basie played the Famous Door from July, 1938 to January, 1939 and it was a mark of Willard Alexander's faith in the band that he loaned the club 2,500 dollars to install air-conditioning to attract the customers during the hot summer months of 1938. Alexander also twisted a few of the most influential arms at CBS with the result that a radio network line was installed. Basie was paid about 1,300 dollars a week at the Famous Door but the extensive radio network coverage was of immense value. The surviving broadcast recordings from the Famous Door are revealing for a number of reasons, not the least being the excellence of Jack Washington as an improvising baritone soloist, at a time when such fluidity on the instrument was the prerogative of Harry Carney, or so it seems judged solely on the evidence of commercially made records. Frank Driggs points out that it was the success and popularity of the contrasting tenor soloists which caused Basie to drop Washington from a prominent role as a soloist. The Famous Door transcriptions show also that Benny Morton was the chief trombone soloist probably because Dicky Wells had only recently come into the band. There is also another example of Lester Young's clarinet playing to add to the discographies. Basie's judicious fill-ins and occasional middle-eights sandwiched between ensemble passages helped to give the band a sense of contrast which few others possessed at the time.

The six month residency at the Famous Door was followed by a further six month engagement in Chicago and these extended bookings gave the band a feeling of stability. The new men had plenty of opportunities to familiarise themselves with the band library and their section colleagues. Record producers also found it useful to have so many outstanding jazz players in one place for so long. John Hammond recorded bands under the leadership of both Billie Holiday and Teddy Wilson during 1938 when the supporting musicians were nearly all

3 The Count Basie Orchestra, circa Spring 1954 with Frank
   Wess and Frank Foster soloing (Melody Maker)

taken from the Basie ranks. Under his own name Count was fulfilling his Decca contract both with the full band and as leader of the 'All American Rhythm Section'. The titles Basie made in November, 1938 and January, 1939 give us rare opportunities to study the magic of this unique team. Hammond had been right in drawing Freddie Green to Basie's attention for seldom in jazz did two musicians complement each other better. The foundation of the team was the immensely strong and authoritative bass playing of Walter Page, a man who knew instinctively how every other instrumentalist in the band should play. Basie credits Page bringing out the best in Jo Jones and it was probably Page's idea that Jones scaled his sound down to the point where the beat was sometimes felt rather than heard. Jo Jones certainly knew how to paint rhythmic colours and was never boorish in his work behind band or soloists. In fact it was Jones who paved the way for the later 'cool school' drummers with his floating rhythmic pulse and beautifully controlled hi-hat cymbal. 'Jo Jones' said drummer Don Lamond, one of the finest of all big band drummers, 'reminds me of the wind. He has more class than any drummer I've ever heard and has been an influence on me ever since I first heard him with Basie. Man, he could drive that band! With Jo there's none of that damn raucous tom-tom beating or riveting-machine stuff. Jo makes sense'. Jones started out as a carnival musician and had to be prepared to accompany all manner of acts and improvise backing at a moment's notice. All this served him in good stead when he came to work with Basie for he had the ability to listen to each soloist, modify his accents as necessary and, at the same time, fit in with the other members of the rhythm team. On Jones's right sat Freddie Green, probably the greatest rhythm guitarist in the history of jazz. He was called, with perfect truth, Basie's left hand. As he explained, 'Basie's piano certainly contributes to making the rhythm smooth. He contributes the missing things. I feel very comfortable working with him because he always seems to know the right thing to play for rhythm. Count is also just about the best piano player I know for pushing a band and for comping soloists. I mean the way he makes different preparations for each soloist and the way, at the end of *his* solos, he prepares an entrance for the next man. He leaves the way open'. Sitting at the keyboard, watching and listening to every move made by his musicians, Basie played with deceptive simplicity. 'I don't want to "run it into the ground" as they say. I love to play, but the idea of one man taking one chorus after another is not wise, in my opinion. Therefore, I fed dancers my own piano in short doses, and when I came for a solo I did it unexpectedly, using a strong rhythm background behind me. That way we figured, the Count's piano wasn't going to become monotonous'. This magnificent and unique quartet of players came into being in March, 1937 and stayed together, week in and week out, until the summer of 1942 when Page left, following a disagreement. It formed the foundation to some of the finest examples of big band swing and was the envy of every other band leader.

While the Count Basie band was still appearing at the Famous Door, John Hammond arranged a concert presentation at Carnegie Hall for December 23rd, 1938. 'The concert should include, I thought, both primitive and sophisticated performers, as well as all of the music of the blacks in which jazz is rooted. I wanted to include gospel music, which I listened to in various store-front churches wherever I travelled, as well as country blues singers and shouters, and ultimately the kind of jazz played by the Basie band'. The two LPs issued years later from the 'Spirituals To Swing' concert are especially valuable for some small band titles by Basie, Lester Young, Buck Clayton and rhythm (even although the tracks on the LP were actually recorded six months earlier in a studio and have fake applause dubbed on) and a reunion between Basie and trumpeter Hot Lips Page. At the commencement of 1939 Decca set up five Basie dates within the space of a month. The recording contract was due to expire and Decca were anxious to retain the services of Basie; they sent Jack Kapp along to Basie with a thousand dollars as an inducement to sign for a further term. Although he needed the money, Count refused to stay with Decca and signed instead with Columbia, an arrangement which was to last in unbroken form until August, 1946. With a new contract for making records, Basie found himself in direct competition with Duke Ellington. Duke's was the only Negro band on the Columbia label 'but because of Ellington's understanding with Columbia' wrote John Hammond later 'Basie's records had to be released on Okeh. When Basie finally moved to Columbia, Ellington left and went to Victor. I never understood the jealousy and resentment Duke seemed to feel toward other black band leaders. His place was secure, his genius recognized, yet he seemed to feel threatened. I do know that Basie worshipped him'. Just prior to the conclusion of the Decca arrangement, Count was faced with the need to find another tenor soloist. The outstanding Herschel Evans collapsed while working with Count Basie at the Crystal Ballroom, Hartford, Connecticut in January, 1939. He was rushed to a New York hospital but died of a cardiac condition. Basie borrowed Chu Berry from Cab Calloway's band to complete his Decca dates then brought in another Texas tenor, Buddy Tate, as a permanent replacement. (Buddy became one of the longest-serving Basie sidemen; he joined the Count in February, 1939 and left in September, 1948.) Although Basie had fostered the 'tenor battles' while Evans and Lester Young sat at opposite ends of the saxophone section, those who were close to the two men claimed that the so-called feuding bore no relation to their true feelings. 'Herschel Evans was a natural' said Jo Jones. 'He had a sound on the tenor that perhaps you will never hear on a horn again. As for the so-called friction between him and Lester, there was no real friction. What there was was almost like an incident you would say could exist between two brothers. No matter what, there was always a mutual feeling there. Even in Lester's playing today, somewhere he'll always play two to four measures of Herschel because they were so close in what they felt about music'. Evans left his stamp on a handful of the Decca sides, notably the gorgeous and sensitive statement on *Blue and sentimental* as well as more aggressive solos on *One o'clock jump, Time out, Georgianna* and his own arrangement of *Doggin' around*. (In all four latter titles Herschel is the first of the two tenor soloists.)

The first session for Columbia took place at United studios in Chicago on February 13, 1939 but none of the titles was issued until 33 years later. 'We cut these in a terrible studio and there was something wrong with the equipment' wrote John Hammond years later. 'When we finally cut the masters we couldn't get the records to track'. This was not a full band session but by an octet, with Jimmy Rushing singing on *Goin' to Chicago*, a track on which Basie played organ. Jo Jones recalls that 'the goddam organ wouldn't work properly and I had to get under it and kick it to make it go. It hadn't been played for close on ten years'. When these titles eventually appeared as part of a two-LP set titled 'Count Basie – Super Chief' the jazz world was suddenly the richer by some magnificent Buck Clayton, Lester Young, Dicky Wells and Basie solos following the painstaking work of recording engineer Doug Meehan who went to endless trouble to overcome the original defects. From what might have seemed an inauspicious beginning, the Columbia contract blossomed into full flower a month later with an orchestra date and the band built steadily on the foundation of this success throughout the rest of the year. As the war clouds gathered over Europe Basie was recording gems such as *Taxi war dance, Rock-a-bye Basie* (a tune which Dizzy Gillespie later claimed was based on one of his riffs which Shad Collins took with him into the Basie band), Jimmy Mundy's arrangement of *Miss Thing* (which was spread across two sides of a 78) and *Jump for me*. Two days after Britain declared war on Germany Count Basie's Kansas City Seven assembled in Columbia's New York studio to record two titles which soon became classics, *Dickie's dream* and *Lester leaps in*. Buck Clayton, Dicky Wells and Lester Young make up an unbeatable front line, superbly backed by the All American Rhythm Section. In the autumn of 1939 Rozelle Claxton (from Ernie Field's band) took Basie's place at the keyboard for a short time while the Count was off sick and the year finished with the band at the Casa Loma Ballroom in St. Louis. *Metronome* magazine asked its readers to vote in its second annual poll with the result that Basie came second on piano, Lester third on tenor and Walter Page, Jo Jones and Freddie Green occupying similar positions on their respective instruments. As a new decade began it looked as if Basie had been accepted, three years after that first booking outside the Kansas City limits. The Count was on his way.

Chapter Four

For much of the first half of 1940 Basie worked around New York and Boston. He was at the Apollo Theatre on at least three occasions and the Golden Gate Ballroom, both venues in New York City, and at Boston's Southland Ballroom, from which latter location an excellent broadcast transcription dating from February 20 has been released on a number of labels. By now the powerful trumpet of Al Killian had replaced Shad Collins and the distinctive Vic Dickenson had joined the trombones, taking the place of Benny Morton who left to join pianist Joe Sullivan's band. In May Milton Ebbins took over as manager from Jack Kearney and Tab Smith was in and out of the band as a fifth saxophonist. The band was still being booked through MCA but Willard Alexander's move to the William Morris agency was having an effect on Count's business. It was not that the band had no work, it was simply that it was not getting the air time which Alexander had considered so important. There have been a few indications that, away from the piano keyboard, Basie's acumen and sense of timing left a lot to be desired. Apart from the unfortunate terms of the Decca contract Basie entered into, the sharp nose-dive of his fortunes with MCA once Alexander left was most noticeable. Both Count and his manager, Milt Ebbins, formally accused MCA of serious charges and the November 15, 1940 issue of *Down Beat* carried the news that Basie felt the agency was guilty of:

a. Failure to book the band into spots with radio wires.
b. General handling of the band: for example it was recently booked for the Paramount Theatre (LA) for two weeks. 'It was the only date we played out there, and it cost us two thousand dollars to send the band there. It doesn't make sense.'
c. Long jumps on tour: 500 miles a night 'not unusual. We've jumped from New York to Chicago in one night'.
d. The band has been a big grosser everywhere it's played (including a recent Southern tour) but 'MCA got some nineteen thousand dollars in commission last year. Basie got seven thousand himself and the band got five thousand. Does that make sense?'

Basie threatened to break up his band, presumably in order to sever his relationship with MCA. Count did a number of one night stands with

Benny Goodman (and played on some of Benny's sextet recording dates) while the rest of the Basie men 'loafed around New York'. Manager Milt Ebbins said he was taking the mismanagement case to James Petrillo, head of the American Federation of Musicians. 'We haven't had a location job with air time for a year. Some weeks we work every night, jumping 500 miles a night. Other weeks we lay off. No one seems interested in Basie at MCA'. By the end of the year an uneasy truce was proposed with MCA taking less commission from the band's bookings. But Basie suffered another setback a couple of weeks before Christmas. Columbia had set up a recording session for Friday, 13th December, 1940 in order to record four titles (*It's the same old South, Stampede in G minor, Who am I?* and *Rockin' the blues*); on the day of the session Basie's star soloist, Lester Young, failed to show up. Rumour has it that he objected to making records on Friday The Thirteenth but those close to the event deny it. In any case Basie was forced, at short notice, to bring in Paul Bascombe on loan from the Erskine Hawkins band, and to allocate the tenor solos on the date to Buddy Tate. It was the parting of the ways, at least temporarily, for Lester and Basie and while the precise reasons for Young's departure may never be known, it is worth recording that Lester's wife, Mary, wrote a letter to *Down Beat* magazine stating the Lester left Basie of his own accord and was *not* fired. Another *Down Beat* report of interest occurs in the January 15, 1941 issue referring to the months of wrangling between Basie and MCA. Count bought his release from the agency for ten thousand dollars and joined William Morris. 'Willard Alexander, Morris band department executive, will personally guide Basie and the band just as he has been doing for the past four years, even though he and Basie were with rival booking offices. Also in the picture is Milton Keith Ebbins, youthful Basie road manager and former band leader, who now becomes personal manager of the Basie outfit. Alexander and Ebbins together will accept or reject all bookings offered. Basie's band hasn't been working much lately. On January 3rd he started a theatre tour, opening at the Apollo in Harlem – the first job to be booked by Morris'. Following the departure of Lester Young, Count used a number of temporary substitutes in his reed section then, at the end of February, 1941, Don Byas took over on a permanent basis.

With Willard Alexander now officially back at the helm the bands fortunes improved. Most of its work was still in ballrooms and theatres where it was expected to provide music not only for dancers but also as the backing for all manner of variety acts and vocalists. What happened

4 Count Basie Orchestra, late 1954 – early 1955 (Melody
   Maker)

in the recording studios was not always necessarily a true reflection of the working band schedule. Jimmy Rushing and Helen Humes were a great success as singers with the band but Helen found the strain of touring too great and left around the time Don Byas came into the band. 'I used to pretend I was asleep on the Basie bus' Helen told Stanley Dance, 'so the boys wouldn't think I was hearing their rough talk. I'd sew buttons on, and cook for them too. I used to carry pots and a little hot plate around, and I'd fix up some food backstage or in places where it was difficult to get anything to eat when we were down South. Playing cards was the best way of passing time on those long trips, but sometimes when I won money from them I found I had to lend it back! I wasn't interested in drinking and keeping late hours, so that part didn't hurt me. But my kidneys couldn't stand the punishment of those long rides. I was too timid to ask the driver to stop when I should have. Then, too, I got tired of singing the same songs year after year'. Miss Humes's eloquent statement tells us more about the reverse side of the show-biz coin than a wealth of conjecture. Life on the road with a touring band has never been good but for girl singers the pressures were greater. Basie brought in Pearl White, a former singer and dancer at the Apollo Theatre in Harlem, as a temporary replacement for Helen and later in the year, Lynne Sherman, one-time vocalist with the Sonny Burke band and now married to Basie's manager Milt Ebbins, sang with the band at an engagement at Boston's Ritz-Carlton. (Lynne also recorded a couple of sides with the band at the end of 1941.) But Jimmy Rushing was still the major attraction in the vocal department, singing the blues and generally giving the band its deeply committed Kansas City sound. Ballads on records were handled by Earl Warren, who was also leading the sax team. The Okeh releases of 78rpm discs usually had an Earl Warren vocal on one side and a more extrovert instrumental number on the other. British EMI, which then had a contract with American Columbia, parent company of Okeh, released Basie records in Britain during World War Two on its Parlophone label and invariably cross-backed the instrumentals, omitting most records with a vocal. One Basie performance with a singer which was issued both in the US and Britain was the two-sided *King Joe*, a somewhat unexpected pairing of the Count's orchestra and the vibrant voice of Paul Robeson. Some of the arrangements for the vocals brought in unexpected names; Hugo Winterhalter, for example, scored some of the Earl Warren features. Basie was also using compositions and arrangements from unusual sources for his instrumentals too; *Stampede in G minor* was written by Clinton P. Brewer, a convicted murderer then serving a 19 year jail sentence while *Beau Brummel* was by the diminutive Margie Gibson. It is likely, however, that many of the titles which the band recorded for Okeh/Columbia were seldom played in public for the band was still working predominantly hotel ballrooms and theatres where the programme of music was certainly less experimental. Years later the same pattern could be observed when comparing the band's recorded output with any listing of tunes played in public. *Metronome* magazine's Bill Coss spent some time travelling with the band at the end of 1956 and his observations are probably typical of almost any period in the orchestra's existence: 'It's interesting to look through the band's arrangements. There are about 180 scores in the libary and, at most, only sixty of these are played. Out of that number, there are perhaps twenty or thirty which are played over and over; the others are mostly dance arrangements, ballads by Edgar Sampson, etc. Of that outside figure of thirty, there are only two or three which have any real musical worth; those the musicans *really* like to play, but they generally have to badger the Count into playing them. Basie doesn't like to play new arrangements. Like most of jazz, like most jazz musicians, the arrangements written and played are of familiar blues and standard tunes. Aside from the fact of sheer boredom and over-familiar material, many of the musicians have an artist's interest in new material; but to no avail. Yet they accept it with fortitude, knowing that that is very much the way it is, turning with a wry smile when I would ask them about any new arrangements being in the book and answering "Yep, there's a new arrangement of *Moten swing*"' Basie, like Duke Ellington, may have felt that he was working for two audiences, those who paid at the door to hear the band 'live' and those who wanted a more permanent reminder of the band on record. During the nineteen-forties the band was recording excellent scores by men such as Jimmy Mundy (*Fiesta in blue, Something new, Feather merchant* etc.), Eddie Durham, Buster Harding, Buck Clayton and, occasionally, Skip Martin, Tadd Dameron and Tab Smith. Most of the writers seemed to write with the established sound of the band in mind. (Perhaps they knew that such scores had a better chance of finding their way into the book!) Basie was very much the leader, rejecting anything which he did not feel was right. Buck Clayton told Stanley Dance '(Count) was nice to work for, but he always knew what he wanted from the band and the arrangers. At the beginning, it used to take us so long to get through the arrangements. We'd have to help guys who didn't do so much reading, but who were great soloists and were accustomed to the head arrangements. The only reason I played all those things with a mute with Basie was because he asked me to, and as he was the leader his wishes were like commands. When I came out of the army I was my own judge and I played like I wanted to. The funny thing about Basie was that he'd ask me to record with a mute, but when we got on one-nighters he'd have me play the same thing open'.

Clayton stayed with Basie until November, 1943 when he was called up by the US Army. The Count's band lost a number of men to the armed forces but there is evidence that the US authorities called more whites than Negroes, proportionately speaking, and some of the white bands of the day suffered greater losses of key personnel than either Basie or Duke Ellington. When the V Disc programme of recordings was launched, Ellington and his men made it clear that they were not prepared to take part, as a protest against the way coloured troops were treated. (The Ellington material which does exist on V Disc is generally from public concerts.) Basie, on the other hand, took part in a number of these sessions, a fact which enables us to hear the development of the band during an extended ban on commercial recordings which commenced on August 1, 1942 and, in the case of Basie's recording company, did not end until December, 1944. During this period a number of important personnel changes took place. Don Byas left and Lester Young took his place, having presumably patched up his previous difference with Basie. Buddy Tate remembers that Byas left after an incident one night when Ben Webster sat in with the Count. 'I never heard anyone sound like that in my life, and all the cats flipped over Ben. Poor Don went across the street and got stoned!' Lester came into the band in December, 1943 and stayed until the following September when the army almost literally took him off the bandstand. Lester had been ignoring his call-up papers, using the excuse that, as a member of a touring band, the papers had not reached him. 'When we opened in Los Angeles that year' recalls Tate, 'there was a sharp young cat there who kept looking at Prez and Jo Jones. That wasn't unusual because they were stars. He sat there drinking whiskey all night, but when we got though he came over and said "You, Lester Young, and you, Jo Jones, I have to serve you with these papers. Be down at the Induction Centre tomorrow morning!" '. Their places were taken immediately by drummer Buddy Rich (who succeeded in playing with Tommy Dorsey in the early part of each evening then with

Basie at ten o'clock) and Artie Shaw, who played Lester's tenor parts on clarinet. This was, of course, only a temporary arrangement until Shadow Wilson and Lucky Thompson, on drums and tenor repectively, joined on a more permanent basis. 'When Lucky arrived, he continued the Byas approach' maintains Buddy Tate. 'Lester had naturally been featured more than me, and Lucky was in his chair. Lucky quit when he decided he wanted to stay on the Coast'. Basie's visits to Los Angeles had given him the opportunity of working in films and as early as April, 1943 *Down Beat* was reporting that 'the Basie band can currently be seen in three films, "Hit Parade of 1943" (Republic), "Reveille With Beverley" (Columbia) and "Stage Door Canteen" (United Artists)'. The following August the band was working on three film assignments at Universal, the Donald O'Connor comedy musical 'Man Of The Family' (also known as 'Top Man'), the Olsen and Johnson sequel to 'Hellzapoppin' titled 'Crazy House' (and sometimes 'Funzapoopin') and a Will Cowan short. But perhaps the most significant event was that on November 5, 1943 Count Basie opened at the Lincoln Hotel in New York for an eight week engagement. On the face of it this may seem fairly innocuous but it was the breaking down of a number of barriers. It was Count's first booking into a New York hotel and the first time the Lincoln had ever played host to a coloured band. No doubt Willard Alexander was the power behind the move and the Lincoln booking was an immediate success. In fact the band returned again later and a number of excellent broadcast transcriptions exist from the Lincoln's 'Blue Room' which indicate that Basie did not have to make any concessions to the hotel guests; numbers such as *Harvard blues, Kansas City stride, Dance of the gremlins* and *Rock-a-bye-Basie* abound.

Chapter Five

World War Two ended in August, 1945 at a time when Count Basie was ensconced on the West Coast, fulfilling engagements at the Casa Manana and Club Plantation as well as a number of theatres. The band came West at the beginning of July and did not return to New York until November when they once again rocked the Lincoln Hotel to its foundations. Clearly Basie was on the crest of a wave of popularity with all manner of audiences, from hotel patrons to service men. The band contained a couple of young men who were destined to go on to greater things. Jay Jay Johnson, then 21 years of age but already a veteran of the Benny Carter orchestra, was in the trombone section along with Dicky Wells, Eli Robinson and Ted Donnelly. Illinois Jacquet, a year or so Johnson's senior, had taken Lucky Thompson's place on what had now become, traditionally, the solo tenor chair. Basie featured them strongly, using Johnson's arrangement of *Rambo* (which featured 16 bars of Jay Jay's solo trombone) and scores such as *Mutton leg* (a Harry Edison tune dedicated to Ted 'Mutton Leg' Donnelly), *The king* and *Stay cool*, all of which had solo choruses by Jacquet. The trumpet section also had two important additions in Joe Newman and the sadly underrated Emmett Berry. By the summer of 1946 the All American Rhythm Section was together again; Jo Jones, out of the army, took over the drum stool from Shadow Wilson while Walter Page and Basie made up whatever differences had caused the rift nearly four years earlier. Records from the period indicate that Count was by no means unaware of the new direction jazz was taking and Henri Renaud, in his invaluable and exhaustive 20–LP compilation of Basie's recordings from the Columbia and Okeh files, discovered a previously unissued version of Tadd Dameron's *Stay on it* recorded by Count in July, 1946, a year before Dizzy Gillespie was to record the same score.

The contract with Columbia was running out and Basie made what may be considered another dubious decision. Let John Hammond, who was then working with the new Majestic company, tell the story: 'My major objective after I joined Majestic was to bring Basie with me and I persuaded Gene Treacy and Ben Selvin to offer him a very good contract. It guaranteed him twenty five thousand dollars a year for three years with a minimum of sixteen sides and albums included. It also contained the provision that if I should leave the company, the contract could be cancelled. Basie was still being booked by the William Morris Agency, although Willard Alexander had left. The agent who ran the office and called the shots for Basie was Sam Weisbord. Basie's personal manager was Milt Ebbins, a man with whom I did not get along too well because I never felt he had Basie's best interests at heart. To this day I have no idea what took place between Ebbins and Weisbord. All I know is that I went to California with the Majestic contract to meet with Weisbord and Basie. When I reached the William Morris office I found Basie had already signed with Victor. I knew RCA Victor would not promote him properly, that it was the end of the Basie band on records, and I said so. But whether Basie was in debt at the time, or Ebbins and Weisbord considered Majestic no place for him, I never discovered the reason for his refusal to sign our contract. The next night Basie and I were on a radio programme together. As we left the studio Basie turned to me and said "John, I've never been so ashamed of myself in my life". He was in tears, and because of the frustration I felt, so was I'. The RCA contract commenced with a recording session in Los Angeles in January, 1947 and was to continue for three years. While there certainly are some excellent records from the period, including some fine small band titles, Jimmy Rushing vocals and a magnificent *Shoutin' blues* which gives some indication of the band's zest, in general Hammond's fears were realised. There are dire vocals and several unsuitable choices of tunes including lacklustre 'cover' versions of other artiste's hits, such as *Open the door Richard*. But the fault was certainly not wholly Victor's. Basie himself seems to have lost his direction, musically speaking, and seemed to be casting around for a new identity. It is easy, with hindsight, to criticise him and to point out that he should have persevered with the style of big band jazz he had created. The fact of the matter is that by 1948 the dancing public had changed and the new clubs wanted the 'new music' of Dizzy Gillespie, Stan Kenton and Woody Herman. Basie, who mixed more with his musicians than any other leader, was probably under a certain amount of pressure in the band coach from sidemen anxious to turn him the way they wanted to go. When Leonard Feather conducted a blindfold test on Basie in the summer of 1947 he found Count very enthusiastic about Gillespie's *One bass hit* ('Sounds like the boss, Dizzy. But Red Rodney plays terrific like that too. Arrangement very interesting – tells a story from start to finish. Four stars') and concluded with the remarks, 'I'm from the old school. I'll take the settled old swing with less notes, things that are really simple – but I like to listen to other types.

41

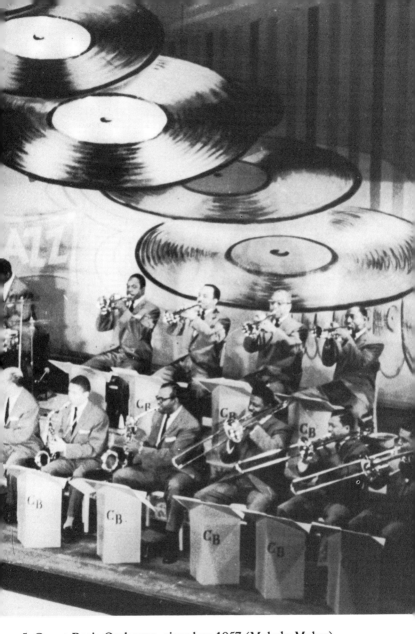

5 Count Basie Orchestra, circa late 1957 (Melody Maker)

The youngsters in my band support the modern part of the music. And I definitely approve of the way jazz is going. As far as bebop is concerned, it's real great if it's played right, and I think it's really taking effect. I have records that I play all the time, trying to understand. Diz and Parker and Jay Jay and Red Rodney – kids like that are really doing it'.

The 'youngsters' in his band at the time included Paul Gonsalves, who had taken over on tenor when Norman Granz made Illinois Jacquet an offer he could not afford to refuse in order to join the touring Jazz At The Philharmonic group. (Jacquet took Joe Newman with him when he left Basie.) By 1948 Count had more 'youngsters' in the ranks including trumpeters Clark Terry and Jimmy Nottingham, Shadow Wilson back on drums and Wardell Gray taking over the principal tenor chair from Buddy Tate. The band was being booked into bop clubs such as the Royal Roost and Bop City rather than the Lincoln Hotel; Jimmy Rushing left to form a small band of his own and by the end of 1949 only a handful of Count's men had been with him for any length of time. Jack Tracy reviewed the band's appearance at Chicago's Blue Note during its December 5 to 11 booking (*Down Beat*, January 13, 1950) and headlined his column 'Basie best of what's left?'. He pointed out that both Woody Herman and Charlie Barnet had been forced to disband due to poor business leaving Basie 'as the best jazz band in the jazz purveying business'. He went on to say that 'the crew is an amalgamation of about every music style in the books. There are Kansas City men Basie, Freddie Green and Dicky Wells; swingsters (Emmett) Berry, Earl Warren, Jack Washington etc. and modernists (Wardell) Gray and drummer Butch Ballard. The rest fall somewhere in between. But this crew is doing quietly and without fanfare just what Dizzy Gillespie made a big issue of – giving the customers bop with a beat, music that is entirely danceable if you want to use it for that'. But Tracy was too optimistic; four weeks after the Blue Note booking Basie broke up his big band and went back to work on February 10, 1950 with a small group. Again the problem stemmed from management and booking; Count had been handled by General Artists Corporation throughout the whole of his RCA Victor contract period and succeeded in getting his release from GAC in January 1950 when he returned to Willard Alexander. It was Alexander who issued a statement saying 'Basie's big band has been badly handled in the last couple of years. It was destroyed as a box office attraction. The small group is a temporary expedient with the current conditions of the band business in mind. The combo might wind up as a

6 The Count in the BBC Studios (Melody Maker)

permanent unit or, if conditions warrant it, he might go back to a big band. It just depends on what will make the most money for Basie'. Vague talk of a possible European tour by the sextet in April, May or September (none of which actually took place) made it obvious that neither Alexander nor Basie had much of an idea of what the future held. The break up of the big band had been due to nothing but failing business. Keeping such a large unit in being obviously caused many headaches and a combination of circumstances made it possible for Basie to pull a sextet together for a 'hand-to-mouth' run of bookings. The group came together because clarinettist Buddy De Franco was put into the unit by his new manager, Willard Alexander. Drummer Gus Johnson, from Chicago, had worked with Count several years before; Basie remembered hearing bass player Jimmy Lewis in Louisville and called him while Clark Terry, the only member of the sextet who had been with Basie's last big band, recommended tenor saxist Bob Graf from his home town of St. Louis. When the group went into the Brass Rail in Chicago on February 10, the patrons, used to 'pantomime acts and cocktail trios' according to *Down Beat* magazine, were fascinated to see, in person, a major name from the worlds of records and films, albeit leading probably the smallest unit he had ever fronted. The sextet became popular (although writers continued to comment on the somewhat strange mixture of styles) and a number of interesting saxophonists passed through the ranks. For a time both Bob Graf and baritone saxist Serge Chaloff worked in the band and each, at that time was undergoing his own personal problems. They literally leaned on Clark Terry as they flanked him in the front line and Clark remarked later that it was no wonder his shoulders developed a permanent slant! Basie brought in Wardell Gray on tenor when he flew out to California for some bookings and Buddy De Franco was 'Crow Jimmed' out of a film short the band made in August, 1950 when they appeared with Sugar Chile Robinson and Billie Holiday. (De Franco played on the film soundtrack but the coloured clarinettist seen miming on screen was Marshal Royal.) Freddie Green, who was not originally re-engaged after the break-up of the big band in January, joined the sextet one night much to Basie's surprise and pleasure. With the RCA contract at an end, Count went back to Columbia who recorded three sessions with the sextet. (Buddy Rich guested on drums on the first one while Charlie Rouse was the temporary replacement for Bob Graf who had left to join the new Woody Herman band.) While the titles made by the small group are delightful, they lack the suppressed power and excitement of any previous Basie recordings and on *Little white lies*, which has one of the greatest of all Wardell Gray's ballad solos, Count comes on like Bill Snyder, a non-jazz pianist then enjoying considerable popularity with his piano-and-orchestra version of *Bewitched*. In January, 1951 De Franco left to form a band of his own and was replaced by Rudy Rutherford. Then, in April, Basie had the chance to put together a sixteen-piece band for a one week engagement at New York's Apollo Theatre. He rushed the band into the Columbia studios to record his first big band sides since August, 1949 including a splendid version of *Little Pony*. Neal Hefti, who shared much of the writing for the sextet with De Franco, provided the scores and the band contained outstanding lead musicians in Al Porcino (trumpet) and Marshall Royal (alto). But there were no other big band gigs in the offing and Count was forced to reduce to a small band again. In fact this became the pattern for the year; a week at Birdland in April with a septet containing guest trumpeter Buck Clayton, then a big band booking at the Strand Theatre the next month.

Basie took a big band to the Oasis Theatre in Los Angeles for two weeks in August then turned up at Chicago's Capitol Lounge in September with a septet. But in October he put together a big band for a week at the Savoy Ballroom and managed to weather the storm for never again did he have to reduce the size of his orchestra. The October, 1951 band contained Gus Johnson, Freddie Green and Jimmy Lewis from the last septet plus a trumpet section containing boppers Tommy Turrentine and Idrees Sulieman. The Lester Young *doppelganger* Paul Quinichette took most of the tenor solos and, thanks to a good humoured subterfuge by Clark Terry in his recommendation to Basie, Ernie Wilkins came into the band as an alto saxophonist. (Unknown to Basie at the time, Ernie had never played alto in his life; he was working around East St. Louis on tenor, his usual instrument, when he got the Count's call for he and his brother Jimmy to come to New York. Ernie's mother borrowed a silver lacquered alto from an amateur musican and Ernie came into the band with what the band called his 'grey ghost'!) This was the band that Basie faced 1952 with, and a somewhat uncertain future it was for most big bands had already gone to the wall. The bright light was a new recording contract, signed with Norman Granz for a three year period (with options), and two sessions lined up in January. Trumpeter Joe Newman came back into the band and the strong trombone section comprised

7 Count Basie (Hans Harzheim)

Henry Coker, Benny Powell and Jimmy Wilkins but perhaps the most important recruit was Marshall Royal on lead alto. Royal had been playing clarinet in the septet and did not expect to remain more than six months in Basie's employ. In fact he was promoted to the position of deputy leader and took many musical responsibilities off the Count's shoulders as well as shaping the saxophone section into one of the very finest teams jazz has ever known. The blend of the five men, their time keeping and their ability to play quietly has been a hallmark of the Basie band since the early Fifties and the major credit must go to Royal. Although he himself is a somewhat sweet-toned soloist he has always known how to get the very best from his colleagues. With the formation of what soon became known as the 'new' Basie band, Royal's role became more exacting than that of any previous lead saxist under the Count's banner. The new band relied more on arrangements than earlier units, giving the section leaders the task of achieving technical perfection and a proper regard for dynamics. The very first titles recorded by Basie under his new contract with Granz called for supreme musicianship on the Neal Hefti arrangements of *Sure thing, Why not?* and *Fawncy meeting you* plus Nat Pierce's masterly *New Basie blues*. The impact of those first Clef recordings on the jazz record scene was comparable with that of the first discs by the 'new' Duke Ellington band (*Fancy Dan, The Hawk talks* etc.) a year or so before. It seemed that Count had found a place for himself in the hierarchy of the jazz orchestras and, fittingly, it was near the very top. All that was needed was a slight adjustment to the solo strength and that was soon to be achieved with the arrival, in May 1952, of the bustling tenor of Eddie 'Lockjaw' Davis. Again Basie had a reed section with two contrasting tenors and a rhythm section as good as ever.

Chapter Six

The new Basie band was a musical success on and off records and did good business around New York but its nationwide tours were disappointing in terms of financial return. The breakthrough came in the summer of 1953 and it was probably coincidental that a change took place in the reed section around this time. Frank Wess joined the band on tenor as a replacement for Paul Quinichette then, a few weeks later on July 27, Frank Foster took over from Eddie Davis and stayed for exactly eleven years. *Metronome* magazine published a very perceptive review of the band at this time: 'This is obviously the way a big band should sound; with an even attack, a brace of excellent soloists, a dedication to the beat and a library of arrangements that permit the soloists and the sections to keep the rhythm going always. . . This is not the incubator of jazz of the future as the first Basie band was. It is unlikely that a Pres will emerge out of this group to shape a whole new era of jazz. This is rather a band that sums up, that shows how it is done and how it is played, what was good and what still is good in the jazz of twenty years ago and of today. In the other arts, it is always those who sum up, who demonstrate the enduring in the past and present, who make the great artists'. The essential rightness of these opinions was to be proved time and again during the next three decades for no barrier-breaking soloist was to emerge from the Basie ranks, rather it was a band which became the curator of jazz big band tradition. During the years Basie spent under contract to Norman Granz the impresario tried to arrange a recording session at which Charlie Parker was to have been featured with the band. (Granz had both men under contract at the time.) Parker refused because, he said, Basie would never let him sit in back in Kansas City in 1936. Count, for his part, probably found the sixteen-year old Parker too wild and unschooled a musician in the Reno Club days; a pairing on record in 1953 or 1954 might well have resulted in some extremely interesting music.

The arrival of Frank Wess was to give the band an additional tone colour for, as well as playing excellent tenor, Frank was a flautist, a not too common 'double' in jazz at the time. In fact Basie was unaware of Wess's second instrument for some weeks. 'It wasn't until Frank had been in the band for some time before Don Redman said to me one night, "Frank played any flute for you yet?" I said I didn't know he played it. So a few nights later I said to Frank, "Why didn't you tell me you play flute?" and he said "you didn't ask me!" so I said, bring your flute tomorrow night'. Thus began a long line of flute features including *She's just my size, The midgets, Flute juice* and *Perdido*. In Frank Foster, Basie had not only an excellent tenor soloist rooted in the Wardell Gray and Sonny Stitt tradition, but also a most workmanlike arranger. In fact the quality of the scores produced by men within the band equalled that of the more experienced outside writers. Neal Hefti, a man with a considerable reputation gained from his work for the Woody Herman Herd, had enhanced his reputation with his scoring for the septet and octet then followed it with more writing for the new big band. Johnny Mandel, who played bass trumpet with Basie from June until December, 1953, wrote about ten arrangements for the Count of which only *Straight life* seems to have been recorded. Manny Albam, Sy Oliver, Buster Harding, Don Redman and Nat Pierce were the most prominent of the 'outside' arrangers. The band recorded material in 1953 which Granz put together as a ten-track album called 'Count Basie Dance Session'; it was greeted so enthusiastically by critics and public alike that 'Count Basie Dance Session No.2' was soon in the shops. The albums were important in two respects, apart from their great musical value. Firstly, the titles showed the public that Basie still considered himself to be the leader of a band which played music for dancing and secondly, the very fact that the LPs were given titles was something of an innovation. Previous Basie albums tended to be made up of 78rpm titles simply programmed as ten-inch or twelve-inch discs. The Count's 'Dance Session' LPs were referred to as such by critics and public both at the time and even years later when the discs were reissued. Subsequently the practice of giving albums generic titles was to become the norm and in Basie's case his best-known LPs, for example 'The Atomic Mister Basie'. 'On My Way And Shoutin' Again' etc., have become part of jazz history.

In March, 1954 Count made his first trip to Europe, touring Scandanavia, France, Switzerland etc. but missing out the United Kingdom due to the lingering dispute between the musicians's unions of the two countries. Back home business was good and the band was finding its feet, financially, but it needed just one extra effort to take it to the top. The missing ingredient was a singer with a commanding personality and on Christmas Day 1954, that singer arrived on stage with the big band for the first time, Joseph Goreed Williams, born in Cordele, Georgia, raised in Chicago, and just two weeks past his 36th birthday. Joe was an immediate success to the point where Granz rushed out his versions of *The comeback* and *Every day* as a 45rpm single suitable for the juke box operators. This was followed by the band's *Alright, okay you win* and *When the sun goes down*, with that rich voice well to the fore. At the recording session in May, 1955 when Williams's hits were taped (Frank Foster and Ernie Wilkins provided the scores) Basie recorded another best selling title, *April in Paris*. This was arranged by organist Wild Bill Davis and it was the original intention for Davis to record it with the band. Unfortunately Wild Bill's vehicle broke down on the way to the studio and what turned out to be a best-selling record was made without him. 'I sure fixed Bill's truck that day!' joked Basie years later. The purists sneered at the Joe Williams vocals and the *April in Paris* record, with its 'one more time' ending and its *Pop goes the weasel* quotation in Thad Jones's trumpet solo but the fact remained that Basie, at long last, had financial stability. The pay roll to keep sixteen men swinging got bigger each year and although the relationship between Count and his men was more cordial, relaxed and closer than that of any other band, it did not prevent the sidemen taking the leader to the union when they felt they had a case on matters such as overtime payments etc. As Nat Hentoff wrote in his revealing essay in his book 'The Jazz Life', 'Basie is quite conservative concerning money. He has to be pressured into giving a rise, and he deals with each man in the band individually in a divide-and-conquer technique that lessens the possibility of mass mutiny with regard to basic pay. This absence of collective bargaining exists in many other bands. Basie was not always so close, but he has been mulcted outrageously in his years as leader'.

With his fortunes now on an upward trajectory, Basie made a change in the band which some of his men disagreed with; he sacked drummer Gus Johnson. 'I was in the band until December 22, 1954' Gus told Stanley Dance. 'On the 23rd, I was in hospital with appendicitis. I was there ten days or so when Basie wrote me to say he had got Sonny Payne and that he was doing a good job. Basie liked a lot of flash, and some of the fellows in the band though Sonny was better than me because he was more of a showman. Charlie Fowlkes told me later on that he (Charlie) fell and broke his kneecap and Basie didn't hire him back either. The same thing happened to Marshall Royal when he had to go into hospital. Moral: Don't get sick!' Sonny Payne, who had worked with the Erskine Hawkins band and was the son of drummer Chris Columbus, was expert at juggling sticks and generally playing to the audience when the occasion demanded (and sometimes when it was not demanded). As Nat Hentoff described Payne, he was 'inclined to send up rockets when the music called for indirect lighting'. He also had a tendency to rush the beat and, for a time, Freddie Greene kept a long stick with which he poked Sonny when the time started to go awry. Gus Johnson was the very finest drummer Basie had, after the departure of Jo Jones, but the employment of a showman on the drum stool was part of the change which the band was experiencing. More and more the bookings were for concerts and less for dancing. Audiences paid to see and hear the band as a band and Basie, who probably recalled those years in vaudeville, loved the reaction of a crowd to pure showmanship. This did not, of course, lower the band's musical abilities in any way, in fact some of the new scores called for a degree of musicianship which previous line-ups would have found too demanding. In 1956 Norman Granz released an album on which Basie and Joe Williams shared equal billing. It was clear that Joe was now one of the band's biggest assets. Most critics damned Williams with faint praise, accusing him of not being a true blues singer and of using material which was weak, pallid and generally unsuited to the context. It is highly likely that Count smiled benignly at such criticisms as he turned to check the full list of bookings which the band was enjoying. To Count, Joe Williams was always 'my favourite son' and it is not difficult to see why he was held in such esteem for his addition to the band moved Basie into a new strata as far as fees for engagements were concerned. In 1956 the band took off on another European tour (again missing out Britiain; the inter-union problem had still to be finalised) and Granz recorded the band in concert at Gothenberg. The resultant LP came out misleadingly titled 'Count Basie In London' but at least it gave us the opportunity of hearing how the band performed in front of an audience. Apart from the expected Joe Williams favourites, the programme also contained a new and attractive work by Frank Foster, *Shiny stockings*, which the band had first recorded in the studio at the beginning of the year. To be fair to Basie, he was also recording more challenging works including the extended *Coast to coast* suite by Ernie Wilkins.

In April, 1957 Count Basie paid his first visit to Britain and met with a most enthusiastic response wherever he played. So great was the demand for the band that arrangements were immediately put in hand to bring Basie back in the October of that year. In between the UK bookings, Count made a considerable impact on the 8,000 audience at

the Newport Jazz Festival. The final concert was held on Sunday, July 7th and for the occasion John Hammond came on stage to effect the introductions. After the regular band had played its opening number a quartet of distinguished Old Boys made their appearance to be featured with the band. Lester Young, Jo Jones, Jimmy Rushing and Illinois Jacquet added their own special magic and excitement to the occasion and on the final *One o'clock jump* trumpeter Roy Eldridge also joined in. Granz taped almost the whole of the Newport Jazz Festival that year and the two albums on which Basie may be heard from this event were the last under his contract with Clef/Verve. In the autumn he signed with the comparatively new Roulette company and commenced his new affiliation with an album of Neal Hefti compositions which, rightly, has become a classic by any standards, 'The Atomic Mr. Basie'. A few days after completing the album the band flew to Britain where they performed a number of the new Hefti works including the slow and beautiful *Li'l darlin'* and the hectic *Whirly bird*. So great was the response and so outspoken were British musicians in their claims that they had no chance to hear the band (as the concerts were held, naturally, while other musicians were working) that a special concert was arranged, commencing at midnight. The Roulette recording contract lasted for five years during which time Basie made some 20 albums for the label, the majority of which are excellent. Not only are they musically brilliant but the recording quality is outstanding, thanks to the experienced Teddy Reig who produced most of the LPs. While the Clef/Verve issues were acceptable some sessions, noticeably those which went into the making of the 'Dance Sessions' albums, suffered from a slight muddiness. With the 'Atomic Mr Basie' the music jumped from the speakers, even in mono, with a degree of separation and perspective which the Count had never previously enjoyed.

Before the European tour in the autumn of 1957 Basie made some changes, two of them to tighten discipline within the band. Bill Graham had been playing alto in the band since the early part of 1955 when he took Ernie Wilkins's place and his departure was not unexpected. As Nat Hentoff tells it 'Billy Graham, an extrovert and prankster, "played himself out of the band" as one of his fellow roisterers puts it. "Billy was not only too playful, but he used to get a little too familiar with the Chief himself. He'd even heckle Basie on the bandstand. As usually happens when a guy goes, Graham got the news during a layoff. When we came back, he just wasn't there" '. The other man to go about the same time was trumpeter Reunald Jones; born in 1910 he was older than anyone else in the band, apart from the Count himself. Hentoff again: 'Seated at the extreme left end of the trumpet section, Jones was always one level higher than his colleagues. He played with one hand, as if in derision of the simplicity of the music. When the rest of the section would rise in unison, Jones invariably remained seated. His expression – no matter how much joking was going on among the men – was constantly sour. Jones's childish campaign of passive contempt was in protest at the fact that Basie never assigned him any solos. Jones was fired finally because, as a section mate says with satisfaction, 'he drank too much water'. Jones was a clubhouse lawyer, and occasionally complained to the musicians's union about overtime matters. He went to the union one time too often'. These two incidents give an insight to the extra-musical problems facing a band leader and although Basie tried to distance himself always from internal troubles, the final decision had to be his. The other side of the coin was the excellence of the music which the band was placing on record for Roulette. Neal Hefti wrote the music for two albums, Quincy Jones another and Frank Foster was responsible for all the music on 'Easin' It'. And Benny Carter, the master of orchestration, came up with two suites, 'Kansas City Suite' and 'The Legend'; on the latter Benny sat in the reed section at the recording session. And the band was recorded 'live' to very good effect at Birdland (with Budd Johnson taking some virile tenor solos) and again down in Miami.

Chapter Seven

The period when Basie was making records for Roulette found the band at its best. Just before the 'The Atomic Mr Basie' album was made, Basie completed 13 weeks in the roof ballroom of the Waldorf-Astoria Hotel in New York City, another 'first', for his was the first big Negro band to play the Waldorf. And in November, 1957 he was chosen to play a Royal Command performance in London. It seemed that Basie was picking up honours in every direction and it is not surprising that his record company was anxious to use the band in some high-powered studio dates. Basie made LPs with Billy Eckstine, Sarah Vaughan and Tony Bennett; (he made two with Bennett, due to a contractual arrangement between Roulette and Columbia, Bennett's record company). Pleasant though these pairings were, they tended to take the spotlight away from the band although one of the best, the first Frank Sinatra–Count Basie LP, was made immediately after the Roulette contract expired. From October, 1962 up to May, 1966 Basie moved easily from the Reprise label to Verve and back again to Reprise. Norman Granz had sold his Verve catalogue to MGM in 1960 and therefore played no part in Basie's recordings during this period. The 'concept' album idea still prevailed with LPs being devoted to the work of individual arrangers or to tunes which had some other connexion. Neal Hefti wrote yet another album ('On My Way And Shoutin' Again' for Verve) and Quincy Jones wrote his second set for Basie ('Li'l Ol' Groovemaker . . . Basie' also on Verve). There was also a preponderance of ephemeral or below standard LPs such as 'Basie's Beatles Bag' and 'Basie Meets Bond' plus a number of albums based on the idea of popular hits played by the band. One curiosity on Verve, titled 'More Hits Of The 50's & 60's' and arranged by Billy Byers, comprised a dozen songs very closely associated with Frank Sinatra (in fact one of the tunes was co-authored by Sinatra) but with no reference to any relationship between the singer and the songs on the album sleeve. A frequent member of the brass section on record at this time was trombonist Urbie Green, although Green does not appear to have played other dates with the band.

Apart from the two Sinatra–Basie LPs for Reprise there were also Verve albums on which the band provided the accompaniment to singers Ella Fitzgerald, Sammy Davis and Arthur Prysock. Compared with the Neal Hefti and Quincy Jones LPs from the period none of the

Basie-plus-vocalists albums was particularly memorable. Away from the recording studio the band was to be found in settings previously denied to it. In his 'Encyclopedia Of Jazz In The Sixties' Leonard Feather noted that 'the band toured the British Isles and the European continent in '61, '62, '63 and '65 and enjoyed a triumphal tour of Japan in May–June, 1963. Basie made motion picture appearances in *Sex and the Single Girl, Made in Paris* and *Cinderfella* as well as TV guest shots with Fred Astaire, Andy Williams, Tony Bennett, Edie Adams, Garry Moore, Frank Sinatra, Sammy Davis, Ed Sullivan and the Bell Telephone Hour'. A number of Basie's most important sidemen and soloists had left the band to go their own way including Frank Wess (who had been switched to alto by Basie when Bill Graham was sacked), Thad Jones and Sonny Payne. On the plus side, Eric Dixon had come into the reed team playing a rich-toned, Lucky Thompson-like tenor plus excellent flute while Eddie Lockjaw Davis came and went a number of times. When he was in the band Eddie could always be relied upon to churn up the excitement without ever going too far into the realms of bad taste for Eddie was, and is, a master of brinkmanship. Not surprisingly many critics express their dissatisfaction and concern about the band's music. Whitney Balliett called it 'Civil Service swing' while John Hammond, who probably felt the change in direction more keenly than most, was obviously hurt by the turn of events.

But worse was to come. In 1966 Basie started recording on a non-exclusive or album-by-album basis and the results were often lacklustre, sometimes downright awful. MCA added a rock guitarist to the band, put pop singer Jackie Wilson in front and came up with an instantly forgettable album titled 'Two Much'. Around the same time the same company put out 'Basie's In The Bag' which mixed current pop tunes (*Hang on Sloopy, Green onions* etc.) with titles such as *Mercy, Mercy, Mercy* and *Let the good times roll*. By comparison the 'concept' albums with self-explanatory names such as 'Broadway – Basie's Way' and 'Hollywood – Basie's Way' seemed to have deep musical significance. Singers of all types still seemed capable of getting Basie to agree to the making of an album, with the result that Kay Starr, the Mills Brothers, Teresa Brewer and the Alan Copeland Singers all appeared on LP with Count. Some interesting soloists cropped up on record with the band at this time, and occasionally worked elsewhere with the band. Roy Eldridge, for example, was with the band from July to September, 1966 (long enough to play on some record dates) while Illinois Jacquet was added for the LP of tunes from 'Half A Sixpence'.

All was not gloom, although the mediocre outweighed the good. Dot, the company which had foisted the Mills Brothers onto Basie for two albums, had the good grace to produce two of Basie's best LPs from the second half of the Sixties and, in so doing, gave prominence to a previously unknown talent who was to play an important part on Basie's arranging staff for some years. This was Sammy Nestico, first cousin of Sal Nistico, the tenor saxist who played with Woody Herman and, later, Count Basie. Sammy Nestico was a trombonist and arranger who served a total of 20 years with the US Air Force and, later, the Marines. He had worked with the Charlie Barnet and Gene Krupa bands before his friend Grover Mitchell, then working in Basie's trombone section, introduced him to the Count. Nestico started writing for Basie in 1968 and the Dot album 'Basie Straight Ahead' was devoted entirely to new works all composed and arranged by Nestico. Sammy obviously grasped the band's strengths immediately and came up with scores which the men seemed to enjoy playing. Moreover, he had the ability to make the band sound the way that audiences identified with Basie. His writing was uncluttered and made equal use of the softer elements (including that million dollar reed section of Marshall Royal, Bobby Plater, Eric Dixon, Lockjaw Davis and Charlie Fowlkes) and the vital, hard-hitting brass. On his first album Nestico came up with a number of very attractive originals, notably *That warm feeling*, cast in the same general mould as Hefti's *Li'l darlin'* and Quincy Jones's *For Lena and Lennie*. The fact that Basie used Nestico's works such as *The magic flea, Straight ahead* etc. in public was an obvious sign of the Count's approval. It was Dot which also sent producer Teddy Reig to Las Vegas in March, 1969 to record the band during their stay at the Tropicana Hotel. Again Reig, aided by engineer Wally Heider, captured the sound of the band to perfection, a band which had its solo strength bolstered by the presence of trumpeter Harry Edison heard here in fine form. The resultant LP, 'Standing Ovation', is one of the great Basie albums of the period and goes a long way towards making up for many previous ephemeral sets. Although there were, deliberately, no new works on the album, the band sounds as fresh as paint, charging through *Broadway, Every tub, The Kid from Red Bank* and *Jumpin' at the Woodside* as if to prove that the library never needed injections from stage musicals or films to make it sound new. As Leonard Feather wrote in his sleeve note: 'the lesson to be learned from a study of these sides is that Basie's hits of the '30s, '40s and '50s are as

viable as ever as we near the end of the '60s. Playing for a hip and receptive audience (Buddy Rich and many of Splanky's old friends were on hand at the Tropicana), the band gave of itself as it always does when there is an occasion to rise to. Given the vast improvement in recording, the presence of such irrestible soloists as Sweets and Jaws, and the enthusiastic ambiance brought about by the situation in which these sides were taped, it is no wonder that Basie and his new legions have managed to prove here that Thomas Wolfe was wrong. Under the right conditions you can indeed go home again, and still have the time of your life'.

Two more albums from the period deserve mention. Bob Thiele produced an unusual LP, not wholly successful, but certainly worthy of any Basie collection. Titled 'Afrique' it brought together the Count and arranger Oliver Nelson for a programme of new music, new to Basie that is. Apart from *Hobo flats* and *Step right up*, both of which Nelson had written originally for an LP by organist Jimmy Smith, there were tunes by avant garde saxophonists Albert Ayler and Pharaoh Sanders. Nelson, an outstanding alto and tenor soloist who made a number of records with Eric Dolphy before he turned to arranging in Hollywood, is the featured alto on Ayler's *Love flower*, a ballad of rare and compelling beauty. *Hobo flats* has Buddy Lucas added on harmonica making it a blues which is even earthier than Basie at his most basic; other tracks have additional percussionists added and although the album, at first sight, may not appear too hopeful it is, nevertheless, an important album as an indication of what the band could achieve in a new direction. Basie himself was pleased with the result although, with his natural modesty, he told John McDonough in *Down Beat* magazine: 'The idea was really Bob Thiele's. He thought we ought to do some of this stuff 'cause we hadn't before. He worked the project out with Oliver Nelson. It was really Oliver's record, you know. But I liked it. He did some wonderful things which we still play. Wanted to do another LP along that line, but something happened. Sure it's different, but I'm perfectly comfortable with it. I like it. A lot of people like it. That's what's most important. Why do people hire me? For what I'm tagged for. But a little flavour of something else won't hurt. It's not ever going to dominate our programme, but it'll always be there to some extent'. The other album to mention represents the opposite end of the spectrum and is generally disregarded by the critics. 'Have A Nice Day', made for the Daybreak label in the summer of 1971 comprises eleven compositions and arrangements by Sammy Nestico. 'Sammy' says Basie on the sleeve 'has a sensitivity, a feel, for our concept that few others have. The thing about him is his feel for the contemporary, the modern. Yet he gets that good, simple, understandable feel of our band as it was when we were first getting started and featuring things like *Every tub, Doggin' around* and *Sent for you yesterday*. An amazing guy!' No barriers are broken here but it is a richly satisfying set which consolidates a lot of the previous work, especially the influences of Neal Hefti and Quincy Jones on the arranging staff. A further plus is the quite superlative recording quality which gives the instruments their correct separation; every strummed chord from Freddie Green comes across with clarity as do the vocalised plunger-muted solos from trombonist Al Grey, one of the most individual and important soloists over the years. And if you want to hear what set Basie's band apart from every other, listen to the superb time-keeping on *Jamie*, a performance which moves sedately along at a shade under eighteen bars per minute.

Away from the recording studios Basie literally embarked on a new venture at the beginning of 1970 when he started a number of annual cruises on the QE2 and also took part in a Caribbean cruise aboard the Rotterdam at the end of 1974. This took place shortly after his 70th birthday which was celebrated in style with a banquet at New York's Waldorf-Astoria. At the end of 1973 he commenced recording again for Norman Granz, who was now running the Pablo label, and this arrangement was to continue until Count's death more than a decade later. Granz had little time for adding unsuitable vocalists or placing the band in a role which made them subservient to a 'concept' programme. He did, however, have an aversion to Freddie Green's rhythm guitar away from the big band setting and the very first dates for Pablo were jam sessions (at which Irving Ashby took Freddie's place) and a trio set with just Basie, Ray Brown and Louie Bellson. Called 'For The First Time' it was just that, for Basie had never previously recorded in a guitarless trio setting. 'That was Norm's idea' Basie told John McDonough in 1975. 'You know it wasn't mine. But it was real fun. In fact we've just finished another trio session with my bass player, Norm Keenan, and Louie Bellson, but this time we added Zoot Sims. It's mostly blues and some other things. Norman Granz is a blues man you know. I guess he didn't want a guitar. For myself, Freddie Green definitely fills out a rhythm section. But there are times we want to play around a little and get loose. Fred keeps you in there, you know – pretty strict'. (Incidentally either Basie's memory was at fault or Granz's information is incorrect; the sleeve of the Pablo Count Basie/Zoot Sims LP lists John Heard as the bass player.)

Norman Granz certainly gave us more of Basie's own playing on record than any previous producer; somehow he found the key which unlocked the Count's aversion to featuring himself. On a number of occasions he teamed Basie with Oscar Peterson and, on the face of it, it would be difficult to imagine two more disparate keyboard players for Basie's style utilised only the notes that actually mattered while Peterson has the greatest command of the piano, in technical terms, since Art Tatum. Yet the duets are brilliant with neither getting in the other's way. Two-piano records are often disappointing but the Peterson–Basie duets are gems of a different kind. Granz also assembled a number of small bands around Basie both in the studio and on the concert platform at various jazz festivals. Typical of the latter is the recording of the spontaneous *Trio blues* (with Ray Brown and drummer Jimmie Smith) at the 1977 Montreux Jazz Festival. This innocuous performance starts quietly then builds in intensity until the crowd is applauding in time with the music. As if to ensure that the musicians maintain the upper hand Count breaks into some excellent stride piano, full of syncopation, and the ragged attempts by the audience to join in drop away, much to everyone's amusement. But after the end of 1976 every performance by Basie was a bonus for the jazz world. He suffered a heart attack in September and while Nat Pierce took over the keyboard and Clark Terry was brought in to front the band in Basie's absence, there were many who wondered if the Count would be seen again as part of the world's most swinging orchestra.

Chapter Eight

The show must go on and show business people are endowed with supernatural powers at moments of crisis. Count Basie came back to work after his heart attack and although he may have slowed down, this was certainly not apparent to those who heard the band after Nat Pierce and Clark Terry relinquished the joint leadership role. In January, 1977, three months after the tragedy, Basie was back in the studio for the recording of the 'Prime Time' album, another of Sammy Nestico's sets of arrangements. (Nat Pierce was on hand for the three dates which went into the making of the LP and Basie had him take over the piano bench on *Ya gotta try*. 'I feel very privileged to be Basie's Number One substitute pianist' Pierce told Stanley Dance. 'That's what *he* told me I was'. Pierce played piano on a number of Basie recordings, usually uncredited; he remembers *There are such things* from the album with Sarah Vaughan and *Tell me your troubles* with Joe Williams.) In Las Vegas the following month Basie got together with Dizzy Gillespie on an album which found the two principals exploring a surprisingly large tract of common ground. And then there was the eternal round of the international jazz festivals with Count playing a very large part at Montreux, both with the full band and at jam sessions. The orchestra now had a new and driving drummer in Butch Miles and an eclectic but commanding tenor soloist in Jimmy Forrest. Forrest could bring an audience to its feet with his quote-filled version of *Body and Soul*. *Metronome* magazine was proved right; the Basie band never again spawned soloists of the calibre found at the Reno Club or the Roseland Ballroom. At the same time it had to be recognised that the band was playing an entirely different set of venues to audiences who were content simply to see a world famous leader and his well-drilled, efficient band in the flesh. This was to become the pattern until the end with the difference that Basie's failing health kept him away from work more than at any time in the past. Yet he struggled manfully to take his place in the rhythm section as much as possible. As Chris Sheridan wrote in his uncredited obiturary in *Jazz Journal*, 'the band held together doggedly through Basie's latter-day periods of convalescence, even when, in the last few years, Basie himself was needing six weeks rest for every four on the road. He fought off a heart attack, pneumonia and, latterly arthritis to continue his musical life'. When he came to Britain for the last time, in

September 1982, he came riding on stage in a motorised wheel chair equipped with a special hooter to announce his arrival. He looked for, and found, the easy way much of the time but, thanks to Norman Granz, we have some exceptional examples of his piano playing both in solo and as an accompanist. On the Basie/Zoot Sims album, for example, there is an animated and two-handed solo on *Honeysuckle rose* following the tenor choruses, as if Count wanted to play his own personal tribute to composer Fats Waller. And in a Las Vegas recording studio on November 1, 1981 Norman Granz put Basie at the keyboard with his so-called Kansas City Six to make music as blues-filled and as timeless as anything he had ever done before. With trumpeter Willie Cook, alto saxist Eddie 'Cleanhead' Vinson, guitarist Joe Pass, bass player Niels Henning Orsted Pedersen and drummer Louie Bellson the clock was wound back to the halcyon days for 40 minutes of superb music.

Basie was the last of the great piano-playing band leaders, outliving Duke Ellington, Earl Hines, Fletcher Henderson, Claude Hopkins and the rest. He would probably not have put himself in that category for modesty was an omnipresent characteristic of this man. Yet he probably achieved more than any of the others as an influence. He showed what could be done with a big band in terms of keeping the dancers happy while still providing musical interest for the dedicated jazz lovers. His time keeping was impeccable and the very mention of his name in a description of someone else's musical style immediately implants an accurate idea in the mind. Some stock arrangements for big bands are still marked 'Basie style' or 'Basie tempo' as a guide to budding musicians anxious to learn the finer points of orchestral jazz. Some of his best performances were heard live, or at least as recordings of a concert event, for they enabled Basie the luxury of getting the tempo right over a series of opening choruses by just the rhythm section. A lasting favourite was *I needs to be bee'd with* written in 1958 by Quincy Jones for the 'Basie – One More Time' album on Roulette. The original studio version opens with a brass shout before leading into one piano chorus which acts as a prelude to Al Grey's solo. A number of 'live' versions, both on record and video, made over the ensuing years, open with as many as nine choruses of rhythm section only before the band makes its appearance. Bill Coss described the way Count eases the band into a performance: 'you'll often see and hear Freddie and the Count playing introductions which may be several choruses long, changing tempos, checking with each other, finding the groove which pleases them most, (Basie smiling with evident

glee and Freddie nodding with sophisticated satisfaction when they reach that point), then the Count's right foot, which is most often wound around the chair until then, kicks out, there is a sound of command and the band is unleashed in all its fury'. Basie himself was probably thinking of the time-restrictions of record-making when he spoke of getting started; 'I don't think that a band can really swing on just a kick-off, you know; I think you've got to set the tempo first. If you can do it the other way, that's something else. Anyway, we do it our way; I set it with Freddie, sometimes for a couple of choruses. That's it, see. We fool with it and we know we've got it, like now'. The simplicity of the statement is typical of the Basie philosophy over the years but so many others have tried and failed; they have found that 'simple is difficult'. The creation of a floating beat, a four-man rhythm section which thinks, breathes and plays as one, is something which has eluded many, even the Basie band itself when Count was absent. Johnny Mandel tells the story about listening to the Basie band rehearse one afternoon while the Count wandered about the empty night club, paying no attention to his band or its playing. The musicians were obviously uncomfortable and they practically forced him to the piano. Suddenly the band smashed right and left as it had not done earlier. That was no reflection on the other three members of the rhythm section. The Basie magic was hard to explain.

Harder to explain was the Count himself for he allowed very few people ever to get close to him. 'No member of the jazz pantheon smiles so much and says so little as Count Basie' wrote Nat Hentoff in 1962. '"Except for Freddie Green nobody really knows Bill" says a veteran member of the band. "He keeps in most of what he feels, and the face he presents to the public is usually the one we see too. Once in a great while he'll explode or do something else that isn't in keeping with the usual picture of him, but he quickly picks up his customary role. And from time to time, we'll see Freddie Green lecturing him off to one side – never the other way around. But I don't know what those conversations are about"'. Basie as leader was unlike any of his contemporaries. For years he travelled in the band bus with everyone else, unlike Duke Ellington, who always travelled in Harry Carney's car or some bandleaders who drove their cars a mile or so behind the band bus to ensure there was no stopping *en route*. Count fostered the happy family atmosphere, a rare commodity in a touring band with all the pressures that that throws up. Buddy Tate says that in all the years he spent with Basie he never once

When his fortunes improved Basie invested money in a 132nd Street and Seventh Avenue club named after him. He also bought a house in St Albans, Long Island, which became home for his wife, Catherine, and their daughter Diane. On the few occasions he was at home he relaxed in front of the television set or operated his model railway layout down in the basement. In an obviously ghosted article in 1955 *Down Beat* he wrote 'Not too long ago there was a real "crazy" dog in our household with a pedigree a mile long and natch we called him "One O'Clock Jump". All house broken and lovable, he was a nice little fella, but we had to get rid of him because he just couldn't get used to the two-legged man of the house, namely me. You see, in the past so many years I just haven't been around home long enough for him to dig me. You know, that darn "mutt" wouldn't let me get past the first crack in the door. But don't get me wrong, I love the road. It may be a little tough on my wife and kid, never seeing their father and husband until Birdland time comes around, but it has and will remain a great thrill and challenge to me'. Like many others, Basie had been around so long that he could not envisage a time when he would fail to answer the band call.

His wife, Catherine, first met Bill Basie when he was touring with the Bennie Moten band. She was one of the dancing Whitman Sisters (although her maiden name was Morgan). They were married for more than forty years and her death, in April, 1983, was a severe blow at a time when Count's own health was at a low ebb. He looked for, and sometimes found, solace and companionship on the bandstand where the roar of the crowd provided a satisfaction equal to none.

We are fortunate that Basie left a huge legacy of recorded work and also enabled a large number of young musicians to develop their talents as soloists. Everyone played better when Basie was at the piano and no band has ever swung more. As an epitaph that sentence tells half of the story. The other half is that Bill Basie brought a warm feeling of happiness to millions.

DISCOGRAPHY

Count Basie commenced his recording career in 1929 and to list details of all known sessions, broadcasts etc. would take a book larger than this. At the time of writing Chris Sheridan is putting the finishing touches to what will certainly be looked upon as the definitive Basie listing. My effort is far more modest. I have concentrated almost entirely on sessions which took place under the Count's own leadership (which accounts for the lack of details on the Bennie Moten dates) and have exercised my editorial prerogative in omitting those albums which, in my opinion, do not illustrate the work of the band as a band. This is my excuse for leaving out LPs devoted to vocalists where the band is reduced to a subservient role. I have also omitted a number of albums which are either too lightweight in content ('Basie Meets Bond', 'Basie's Beatles Bag', 'The Happiest Millionaire' etc.) or albums from his most productive periods which do little to add to the band's reputation. For the preparation of this listing I have used the standard discographical works and am most grateful for the late Jorgen Jepsen's 'Jazz Records', 'Count Basie 1929–1950' by Bo Scherman and Carl A. Hallstrom and G. Braun's 'Bielfelder Katalogue 1982'. Tony Shoppee was also of considerable assistance in checking my manuscript. Any resultant errors are entirely mine not Tony's.

The instrumental abbreviations are as follows: – (arr) arranger, (as) alto saxophone, (b) bass, (bs) baritone saxophone, (cl) clarinet, (d) drums, (f) flute, (g) guitar, (org) organ, (p) piano, (perc) percussion, (ss) soprano saxophone, (tb) trombone, (tp) trumpet, (ts) tenor saxophone, (v) and (vcl) vocal.

ALUN MORGAN, *Gillingham, June 1984*

JONES-SMITH INCORPORATED

Carl 'Tatti' Smith (tp), Lester Young (ts), Count Basie (p), Walter Page (b), Jo Jones (d), Jimmy Rushing (vcl).   *Chicago, October 9, 1936*
SHOE SHINE BOY (two takes)/EVENIN' vJR/BOOGIE WOOGIE vJR/OH! LADY BE GOOD **(1)**
(*Note* – in the book 'John Hammond On Record' the date for this session is given as November 9, 1936.)

COUNT BASIE AND HIS ORCHESTRA

Buck Clayton, Joe Keyes, Carl 'Tatti' Smith (tp), George Hunt, Dan Minor (tb),
Caughey Roberts (as), Lester Young, Herschel Evans (ts), Jack Washington (bs, as),
Count Basie (p), Claude 'Fiddler' Williams (g), Walter Page (b), Jo Jones (d), Jimmy
Rushing (vcl).   *NYC, January 21, 1937*

HONEYSUCKLE ROSE/PENNIES FROM HEAVEN vJR/SWINGING AT THE DAISY CHAIN/
ROSELAND SHUFFLE **(2)**

'Chatterbox', Hotel William Penn, Pittsburgh, February 8, 1937

MOTEN SWING (theme)/LADY BE GOOD/ROSELAND SHUFFLE (mistitled SHOE SHINE
SWING)/ST. LOUIS BLUES vJR into MOTEN SWING **(3)**

same location, February 10,1937

MOTEN SWING (theme)/KING PORTER STOMP/I'LL ALWAYS BE IN LOVE WITH YOU/YOU
DO THE DARNDEST THINGS, BABY vJR/SWINGING AT THE DAISY CHAIN/YEAH MAN
(incomplete)/RIFFIN' (mistitled RUG CUTTERS SWING) **(3)**

same location, February 12, 1937

TATTERSFIELD STOMP/LADY BE GOOD **(3)**

Buck Clayton, Ed Lewis, Bobby Moore (tp), George Hunt, Dan Minor (tb), Caughey
Roberts (as), Lester Young, Herschel Evans (ts), Jack Washington (bs, as), Count Basie
(p), Freddie Green (g), Walter Page (b), Jo Jones (d). Jimmy Rushing (vcl).

NYC, March 26, 1937

EXACTLY LIKE YOU vJR/BOO-HOO vJR/THE GLORY OF LOVE/BOOGIE WOOGIE (I MAY BE
WRONG) vJR **(2)**

Earl Warren (cl, as) replaces Caughey Roberts. Add Billie Holiday (vcl).

Broadcast, Savoy Ballroom, NYC, June 30, 1937

MOTEN SWING/SHOUT AND FEEL IT/THE YOU AND ME THAT USED TO BE vJR/THE
COUNT STEPS IN/THEY CAN'T TAKE THAT AWAY FROM ME vBH/I'LL ALWAYS BE IN LOVE
WITH YOU/WHEN MY DREAM BOAT COMES HOME vJR/SWING BROTHER SWING vBH/
BUGLE BLUES/I GOT RHYTHM   Phontastic NOST 7639

omit Billie Holiday.   *NYC, July 7, 1937*

SMARTY/ONE O'CLOCK JUMP/LISTEN MY CHILDREN vJR/JOHN'S IDEA **(2)**

Earl Warren (as, vcl), Eddie Durham (tb, g) added.   *NYC, August 9, 1937*

GOOD MORNING BLUES (two takes) vJR/OUR LOVE WAS MEANT TO BE vEW/TIME OUT/
TOPSY **(2)**

Benny Morton (tb) replaces Hunt.   *NYC, October 13, 1937*

I KEEP REMEMBERING vJR/OUT THE WINDOW/DON'T YOU MISS YOUR BABY?vJR/LET ME
DREAM vEW **(2)**

Buck Clayton, Ed Lewis, Karl George (tp), Bennie Morton, Dan Minor, Eddie
Durham (tb), Earl Warren (as), Lester Young, Herschel Evans (ts), Jack Washington
(bs, as), Count Basie (p), Freddie Green (g), Walter Page (b), Jo Jones (d), Jimmy
Rushing (vcl).   *NYC, January 3, 1938*

GEORGIANNA v JR/BLUES IN THE DARK vJR **(2)**

Harry Edison (tp) replaces Karl George.   *NYC, February 16, 1938*

SENT FOR YOU YESTERDAY vJR/EVERY TUB/NOW WILL YOU BE GOOD?vJR/SWINGIN' THE
BLUES **(2)**

COUNT BASIE QUINTET
Buck Clayton (tp), Lester Young (ts, cl), Count Basie (p), Walter Page (b), Jo Jones (d), Helen Humes (vcl)   *NYC, June 3, 1938*
ALLEZ OOP **(4)**/BLUES WITH HELEN vHH **(4)**/I AIN'T GOT NOBODY –1**(4)**/DON'T BE THAT WAY **(4)**/SONG OF THE WANDERER vHH/MORTGAGE STOMP and six titles on
Phontastic NOST 7639
Note – ALLEZ OOP as MORTGAGE STOMP on **(4)**. The titles from this session which appear on **(4)** have fake applause dubbed on to give the impression they were recorded at Carnegie Hall. Omit Clayton and Young on –1.

COUNT BASIE AND HIS ORCHESTRA
Lester Young (cl, ts). Remainder as before.   *NYC, June 6, 1938*
MAMA DON'T WANT NO PEAS AND RICE vJR/BLUE AND SENTIMENTAL/DOGGIN' AROUND **(2)**

Dicky Wells (tb) replaces Durham.   *Broadcast, Famous Door, NYC, August 9, 1938*
ONE O'CLOCK JUMP (theme)/KING PORTER STOMP   Jazz Archives JA-41

same location, August 12, 1938
I HAVEN'T CHANGED A THING vHH   Jazz Archives JA-41

NYC, August 22, 1938
STOP BEATIN' ROUND THE MULBERRY BUSH vJR/LONDON BRIDGE IS FALLING DOWN vJR/TEXAS SHUFFLE/JUMPIN' AT THE WOODSIDE **(2)**

Broadcast, Famous Door, NYC, August 24, 1938
NAGASAKI/DOGGIN'AROUND   Jazz Archives JA-41

same location, September 6, 1938
INDIANA/OUT OF THE WINDOW   Jazz Archives JA-41

same location, September 13, 1938
WA-TA-TA/INDIANA (incomplete)/LOVE OF MY LIFE vHH/JOHN'S IDEA (incomplete)
Jazz Archives JA-41

same location, October 9, 1938
YEAH MAN   Jazz Archives JA-41

COUNT BASIE QUARTET
Count Basie (p), Freddie Green (g), Walter Page (b), Jo Jones (d)
NYC, November 9, 1938
HOW LONG BLUES/THE DIRTY DOZENS/HEY LAWDY MAMA/THE FIVES/BOOGIE WOOGIE **(2)**

COUNT BASIE AND HIS ORCHESTRA
Ed Lewis, Harry Edison, Buck Clayton (tp), Dicky Wells, Dan Minor, Benny Morton (tb), Earl Warren (as), Lester Young, Herschel Evans (ts), Jack Washington (bs, as), Count Basie (p), Freddie Green (g), Walter Page (b), Jo Jones (d), Jimmy Rushing, Helen Humes (vcl).   *NYC, November 16, 1938*
DARK RAPTURE vHH/SHORTY GEORGE/THE BLUES I LIKE TO HEAR vJR/DO YOU WANNA JUMP CHILDREN? vJR/PANASSIE STOMP **(2)**

74

Add Lester 'Shad' Collins and Hot Lips Page (tp).

Concert, Carnegie Hall, NYC, December 23, 1938

ONE O'CLOCK JUMP/BLUES WITH LIPS/RHYTHM MAN **(4)**

Omit Hot Lips Page. Remainder as before. *NYC, January 5, 1939*

MY HEART BELONGS TO DADDY vHH/WING FOR YOUR SUPPER vHH **(2)**

COUNT BASIE QUARTET

Count Basie (p), Freddie Green (g), Walter Page (b), Jo Jones (d).

NYC, January 25 & 26, 1939

OH RED/FARE THEE HONEY FARE THEE WELL (two takes)/DUPREE BLUES/WHEN THE
SUN GOES DOWN (two takes)/RED WAGON **(2)**

COUNT BASIE AND HIS ORCHESTRA

Shad Collins (tp), Lester Young (ts), Count Basie (p), Freddie Green (g), Walter Page
(b), Jo Jones(d), Jimmy Rushing (vcl). *NYC, February 2, 1939*
YOU CAN DEPEND ON ME vJR **(2)** Affinity AFS1010

Ed Lewis, Shad Collins, Buck Clayton, Harry Edison (tp), Dicky Wells, Benny
Morton, Dan Minor (tb), Earl Warren (as), Lester Young, Chu Berry (ts), Jack
Washington (bs, as), Count Basie (p), Freddie Green (g), Walter Page (b), Jo Jones (d),
Helen Humes (vcl). *NYC, February 3, 1939*
CHEROKEE PARTS 1 & 2/BLAME IT ON MY LAST AFFAIR vHH **(2)**

Add Jimmy Rushing (vcl). *NYC, February 4, 1939*

JIVE AT FIVE –1/THURSDAY vHH/EVIL BLUES/LADY BE GOOD **(2)**

–1, omit Benny Morton, Dan Minor, Earl Warren and Chu Berry on this track.

BASIE'S BAD BOYS

Buck Clayton, Shad Collins (tp), Dicky Wells (tb), Lester Young (cl, ts), Count Basie
(p, org), Freddie Green (g), Walter Page (b), Jo Jones (d), Jimmy Rushing (vcl).

Chicago, February 13, 1939

I AIN'T GOT NOBODY/GOIN' TO CHICAGO vJR/LIVE AND LOVE TONIGHT/LOVE ME OR
LEAVE ME **(1)**

COUNT BASIE AND HIS ORCHESTRA

Ed Lewis, Buck Clayton, Harry Edison, Shad Collins (tp), Dicky Wells, Benny
Morton, Dan Minor (tb), Earl Warren (as), Lester Young, Buddy Tate (ts), Jack
Washington (bs, as), Count Basie (p), Freddie Green (g), Walter Page (b), Jo Jones (d),
Jimmy Rushing, Helen Humes (vcl). *NYC, March 19, 1939*
WHAT GOES UP MUST COME DOWN (two takes) vJR/ROCK-A-BYE BASIE/BABY DON'T
TELL ON ME (two takes)vJR/IF I COULD BE WITH YOU (two takes)vHH/TAXI WAR DANCE
(two takes) **(1)**

NYC, March 20, 1939

DON'T WORRY ABOUT ME (two takes) vHH/JUMP FOR ME **(1)**

NYC, April 5, 1939

AND THE ANGELS SING vHH/IF I DIDN'T CARE vHH/TWELFTH STREET RAG/MISS THING
(Parts 1 & 2) **(1)**

Chicago, May 19, 1939
LONESOME MISS PRETTY/BOLERO AT THE SAVOY vHH/NOBODY KNOWS vJR –1/POUND CAKE **(1)**

–1, Basie plays organ on this track

Broadcast, Hotel Sherman, Chicago, June 5, 1939
MOTEN SWING/JUMP FOR ME/DARKTOWN STRUTTERS BALL   Jazz Archives JA-41

Chicago, June 24, 1939
YOU CAN COUNT ON ME (two takes) vHH/YOU AND YOUR LOVE vHH/HOW LONG BLUES (two takes) vJR/SUB-DEB BLUES vHH **(1)**

Broadcast, Famous Door, NYC, Summer, 1939
ROCK-A-BYE-BASIE   Jazz Archives JA-41

NYC, August 4, 1939
MOONLIGHT SERENADE vHH/SONG OF THE ISLANDS/I CAN'T BELIEVE THAT YOU'RE IN LOVE WITH ME vJR/CLAP HANDS HERE COMES CHARLIE **(1)**

COUNT BASIE'S KANSAS CITY SEVEN
Buck Clayton (tp), Dicky Wells (tb), Lester Young (ts), Count Basie (p), Freddie Green (g), Walter Page (b), Jo Jones (d)   *NYC, September 5, 1939*
DICKIE'S DREAM (four takes)/LESTER LEAPS IN (two takes) **(1)**

COUNT BASIE AND HIS ORCHESTRA
Personnel as March, 19, 1939.   *NYC, November 6, 1939*
THE APPLE JUMP/I LEFT MY BABY vJR/RIFF INTERLUDE/VOLCANO **(1)**

NYC, November 7, 1939
BETWEEN THE DEVIL AND THE DEEP BLUE SEA vHH/HAM'N'EGGS/HOLLYWOOD JUMP/ SOMEDAY SWEETHEART vHH **(1)**

JAM SESSION
Previous full band personnel plus the BENNY GOODMAN SEXTET; Benny Goodman (cl), Fletcher Henderson (p), Charlie Christian (g), Lionel Hampton (vib), Artie Bernstein (b), Nick Fatool (d) plus Albert Ammons, Pete Johnson, Meade Lux Lewis (p)   *Concert, Carnegie Hall, NYC, December 24, 1939*
LADY BE GOOD **(4)**

COUNT BASIE AND HIS ORCHESTRA
Ed Lewis, Buck Clayton, Harry Edison, Al Killian (tp), Vic Dickenson, Dan Minor, Dicky Wells (tb), Earl Warren (as), Lester Young, Buddy Tate (ts), Jack Washington (bs, as), Count Basie (p), Freddie Green (g), Walter Page (b), Jo Jones (d), Helen Humes, Jimmy Rushing (vcl).
Broadcast, Southland Cafe, Boston, February 20, 1940
ONE O'CLOCK JUMP/EBONY RHAPSODY/RIFF INTERLUDE/DARN THAT DREAM vHH/ TAKE IT PRES/BABY DON'T TELL ON ME vJR/IF I COULD BE WITH YOU vHH/I GOT RHYTHM **(5)**   *NYC, March 19, 1940*

I NEVER KNEW/TICKLE TOE/LET'S MAKE HEY WHILE THE MOON SHINES (two takes)/ LOUISIANA (two takes) **(1)**

76

EASY DOES IT/LET ME SEE (two takes)/BLUES (I STILL THINK OF HER) vJR–1/SOMEBODY STOLE MY GAL vJR–2
–1, trumpets, Buddy Tate (ts) and rhythm only; –2, Harry Edison (tp), Jack Washington (bs) and rhythm only.

Personnel as for February 20, 1940 plus Tab Smith (as)　　*NYC, May 31, 1940*
BLOW TOP (two takes)/GONE WITH 'WHAT' WIND (two takes)/SUPER CHIEF/YOU CAN'T RUN AROUND vJR **(1)**

Omit Tab Smith.　　　　　　　　　　　　　　　　*Chicago, August 8, 1940*
EVENIN' vJR/THE WORLD IS MAD PARTS 1 & 2/MOTEN SWING/IT'S TORTURE vHH/I WANT A LITTLE GIRL vJR **(1)**

NYC, October 30, 1940
ALL OR NOTHING AT ALL vHH/THE MOON FELL IN THE RIVER (two takes) vHH/WHAT'S YOUR NUMBER? (three takes)/DRAFTIN' BLUES (four takes) vJR **(1)**

NYC, November 19,1940
FIVE O'CLOCK WHISTLE (three takes)/LOVE JUMPED OUT (three takes)/MY WANDERIN' MAN (three takes)vHH/BROADWAY (two takes) **(1)**

Previous personnel but Paul Bascombe (ts) replaces Lester Young. Tab Smith (as) added.
NYC, December 13, 1940
IT'S THE SAME OLD SOUTH (three takes) vJR/STAMPEDE IN G MINOR (three takes)/WHO AM I? vHH/ROCKIN' THE BLUES (two takes) **(1)**

Ed Cuffee (tb) replaces Dickenson.　　　　　　　*NYC, January 20, 1941*
IT'S SQUARE BUT IT ROCKS (four takes) vHH/I'LL FORGET vHH **(1)**

NYC, January 21, 1941
YOU LIED TO ME vHH/WIGGLE WOOGIE (two takes)/BEAU BRUMMEL (four takes) **(1)**

Ed Lewis, Al Killian, Harry Edison, Buck Clayton (tp), Ed Cuffee, Dicky Wells, Dan Minor (tb), Earl Warren (as), Tab Smith (as, ss), Don Byas, Buddy Tate (ts), Jack Washington (bs); Count Basie (p), Freddie Green (g), Walter Page (b), Jo Jones (d), Jimmy Rushing, Helen Humes (vcl).　　　　　　*NYC, January 28, 1941*
MUSIC MAKERS (two takes)/JUMP THE BLUES AWAY (two takes)/DEEP IN THE BLUES vHH/JITTERS (three takes)/TUESDAY AT TEN/UNDECIDED BLUES vJR **(1)**

Chicago, April 10, 1941
I DO MEAN YOU/9.20 SPECIAL (two takes)–1/H & J (two takes)/FEEDIN'THE BEAN –1/GOIN' TO CHICAGO vJR **(1)**/FEEDIN' THE BEAN (different take)–1 **(6)**
–1, add Coleman Hawkins (ts) on these titles.

Kenny Clarke (d) replaces Jo Jones. Earl Warren (as, vcl).　　*NYC, May 21, 1941*
YOU BETCHA MY LIFE (three takes)vEW/DOWN, DOWN, DOWN (three takes)/TUNE TOWN SHUFFLE (three takes)–1/I'M TIRED OF WAITING FOR YOU vJR –1
–1, Jo Jones (d) replaces Kenny Clarke. **(1)**

Ed Lewis, Al Killian, Harry Edison, Buck Clayton (tp), Ed Cuffee, Robert Scott, Eli Robinson (tb), Earl Warren (as, vcl), Tab Smith (as, ss), Buddy Tate, Don Byas (ts), Jack Washington (bs), Count Basie (p), Freddie Green (g), Walter Page (b), Jo Jones (d), Jimmy Rushing (vcl). *NYC, July 2, 1941*
ONE-TWO-THREE-O'LAIRY (four takes) vJR/BASIE BOOGIE (three takes)/FANCY MEETING YOU v EW/DIGGIN' FOR DEX (three takes) **(1)**

Dicky Wells (tb) replaces Ed Cuffee. Add Lynne Sherman (vcl).
NYC, September 24, 1941
MY OLD FLAME (two takes) vLS **(1)**/FIESTA IN BLUE (five takes) **(6)**/TOM THUMB **(6)**/ TAKE ME BACK BABY vJR **(6)**

PAUL ROBESON WITH COUNT BASIE AND HIS ORCHESTRA
add Paul Robeson (vcl) *NYC, October 1, 1941*
KING JOE PARTS 1 & 2 (two takes of each part) **(6)**

COUNT BASIE AND HIS ORCHESTRA
omit Robeson. Same session
MOON NOCTURNE vEW/SOMETHING NEW (two takes) vEW **(6)**

NYC, November 3, 1941
I STRUCK A MATCH IN THE DARK vEW/PLATTERBRAINS (three takes)/ALL OF ME (three takes) vLS **(6)**

NYC, November 17, 1941
FEATHER MERCHANT (three takes)/DOWN FOR DOUBLE (two takes)/MORE THAN YOU KNOW (two takes) vLS/HARVARD BLUES (two takes) vJR/COMING OUT PARTY (two takes) **(6)**

Ed Lewis, Al Killian, Harry Edison, Buck Clayton (tp), Robert Scott, Eli Robinson, Dicky Wells (tb), Earl Warren (as, vcl), Tab Smith (as), Don Byas, Buddy Tate (ts), Jack Washington (bs), Count Basie (p), Freddie Green (g), Walter Page (b), Jo Jones (d), Jimmy Rushing, Henry Nemo (vcl). *NYC, January 21, 1942*
ONE O'CLOCK JUMP (two takes)/BLUE SHADOWS AND WHITE GARDENIAS vEW/'AY NOW (three takes) vHN/FOR GOOD OF YOUR COUNTRY (two takes) vJR **(6)**

Jerry Blake (as) replaces Tab Smith. *Chicago, April 3, 1942*
BASIE BLUES (two takes)/I'M GONNA MOVE TO THE OUTSKIRTS OF TOWN vJR/TIME ON MY HANDS vEW **(6)**

COUNT BASIE AND HIS ALL-AMERICAN RHYTHM SECTION
Count Basie (p), Freddie Green (g), Walter Page (b), Jo Jones (d)
Hollywood, July 24, 1942
HOW LONG BLUES/ROYAL GARDEN BLUES –1/BUGLE BLUES –1/SUGAR BLUES –1/ FAREWELL BLUES/CAFE SOCIETY BLUES/WAY BACK BLUES/ST. LOUIS BLUES –1 –1, add Buck Clayton (tp) and Don Byas (ts). **(6)**

COUNT BASIE AND HIS ORCHESTRA

Personnel as for January 21, 1942 but Caughey Roberts (as) replaces Tab Smith

Hollywood, July 27, 1942

RUSTY DUSTY BLUES vJR/RIDE ON vEW/LOST THE BLACKOUT BLUES vJR/TIME ON MY
HANDS vEW/IT'S SAND MAN/AIN'T IT THE TRUTH? (three takes)/FOR THE GOOD OF
YOUR COUNTRY vJR **(6)**

Note – following a disagreement between the American Federation of Musicians and
the recording companies, a ban on commercial recording existed in the United States
starting on August 1, 1942. Despite this, recordings did take place either unofficially or
with the agreement of the AFM for the production of V Discs issued only to the armed
services. Count Basie and his orchestra made a number of such V Discs, most of which
have been conveniently reissued as a double-LP set on the French Festival label. This
album, together with various LPs on labels such as Swinghouse and First Heard,
enables us to study the band's output during the period, a period which saw the return
of Lester Young to the Basie sax section from December, 1943 to September, 1944.
Columbia, Basie's recording company, did not come to terms with the AFM until the
end of 1944. In the meantime Count acted as a sideman on two dates for small
independent labels.

COUNT BASIE AND HIS ORCHESTRA

Buck Clayton, Harry Edison, Ed Lewis, Snooky Young (tp), Eli Robinson, Buster
Scott, Louis Taylor, Dicky Wells (tb), Earl Warren, Jimmy Powell (as), Don Byas,
Buddy Tate (ts), Jack Washington (bs), Count Basie (p), Freddie Green (g), Rodney
Richardson (b), Jo Jones (d).   *Hollywood, early July, 1943*
DANCE OF THE GREMLINS/GI STOMP   Festival Album (F) 147

KANSAS CITY SEVEN

Buck Clayton (tp), Dicky Wells (tb), Lester Young (ts), Count Basie (p), Freddie Green
(g), Rodney Richardson (b), Jo Jones (d).   *NYC, March 22, 1944*
AFTER THEATRE JUMP/SIX CATS AND A PRINCE/LESTER LEAPS AGAIN –1/DESTINATION
KC (two takes)   Mercury (Eu) 6336 346
–1, omit Clayton and Wells

LESTER YOUNG QUINTET

Lester Young (ts), Count Basie (p), Freddie Green (g), Rodney Richardson (b), Jo
Jones (d)   *NYC, May 1, 1944*
BLUE LESTER/GHOST OF A CHANCE (two takes)/INDIANA (two takes)/JUMP LESTER
JUMP   Savoy SJL2202

COUNT BASIE AND HIS ORCHESTRA

Harry Edison, Al Killian, Ed Lewis, Joe Newman (tp), Ted Donnelly, Eli Robinson,
Louis Taylor, Dicky Wells (tb), Jimmy Powell, Earl Warren (as), Lester Young, Buddy
Tate (ts), Rudy Rutherford (bs, cl), Count Basie (p), Freddie Green (g), Rodney
Richardson (b), Jo Jones (d), Jimmy Rushing (vcl)   *NYC, May 27, 1944*
KANSAS CITY STRIDE/BEAVER JUNCTION/CIRCUS IN RHYTHM/GEE BABY AIN'T I GOOD
TO YOU vJR/BASIE STRIDES AGAIN (ALONG AVENUE C)   Festival Album (F) 147

Shadow Wilson (d) and Lucky Thompson (ts) replace Jones and Young.

NYC, October 30, 1944
HARVARD BLUES vJR   Festival Album (F) 147

Harry Edison, Al Killian, Al Stearns, Joe Newman (tp), Ted Donnelly, Eli Robinson, Louis Taylor, Dicky Wells (tb), Jimmy Powell, Earl Warren (as), Buddy Tate, Lucky Thompson (ts), Rudy Rutherford (bs, cl), Count Basie (p), Freddie Green (g), Rodney Richardson (b), Shadow Wilson (d), Jimmy Rushing, Thelma Carpenter (vcl).

NYC, December 6, 1944

TAPS MILLER/JIMMY'S BLUES (two takes) vJR/I DIDN'T KNOW ABOUT YOU vTC/RED BANK BOOGIE (two takes) **(6)**

Ed Lewis(tp) replaces Al Stearns. *NYC, January 11, 1945*
TAPS MILLER/JIMMY'S BLUES vJR/TAKE ME BACK BABY vJR/PLAYHOUSE NO.2 STOMP/ JUST AN OLD MANUSCRIPT/ON THE UPBEAT Festival Album (F) 147

Personnel as for December 6, 1944 *NYC, February 26, 1945*
AVENUE C (four takes)/THIS HEART OF MINE vLS –1/THAT OLD FEELING (two takes) vLS –1 **(6)**
–1, add string section on these titles

Buck Clayton, Harry Edison, Karl George, Ed Lewis, Snooky Young (tp), Ted Donnelly, Jay Jay Johnson, Eli Robinson, Dicky Wells (tb), Jimmy Powell, Earl Warren (as), Buddy Tate, Lucky Thompson (ts), Rudy Rutherford (bs, cl), Count Basie (p), Freddie Green (g), Rodney Richardson (b), Shadow Wilson (d), Jimmy Rushing (vcl) *NYC, May 14, 1945*
HIGH TIDE/SENT FOR YOU YESTERDAY vJR/JIMMY'S BOOGIE WOOGIE vJR/SAN JOSE/B FLAT BLUES Festival Album (F) 147

Emmett Berry, Harry Edison, Snooky Young, Ed Lewis (tp), Ted Donnelly, Jay Jay Johnson, Eli Robinson, Dicky Wells (tb), Preston Love, George Dorsey (as), Buddy Tate, Illinois Jacquet (ts), Rudy Rutherford (bs, cl), Count Basie (p), Freddie Green (g), Rodney Richardson (b), Shadow Wilson (d), Jimmy Rushing, Ann Moore (vcl).

Hollywood, October 9, 1945

BLUE SKIES vJR/JIVIN' JOE JACKSON vAM/HIGH TIDE (three takes)/QUEER STREET (three takes) **(6)**

Emmett Berry, Harry Edison, Joe Newman, Ed Lewis (tp), Ted Donnelly, Jay Jay Johnson, Eli Robinson, George Matthews (tb), Jimmy Powell, Preston Love (as), Buddy Tate, Illinois Jacquet (ts), Rudy Rutherford (bs, cl), Count Basie (p), Freddie Green (g), Rodney Richardson (b), Shadow Wilson (d), Jimmy Rushing (vcl).

NYC, January 9, 1946

PATIENCE AND FORTITUDE (three takes) vJR/THE MAD BOOGIE (four takes) **(6)**

Earl Warren (as) and Jo Jones (d) replace Preston Love and Shadow Wilson.

NYC, February 6, 1946

LAZY LADY BLUES (three takes) vJR/RAMBO (four takes)/STAY COOL (three takes)/THE KING (three takes) **(6)**

Joe Newman, Emmett Berry, Snooky Young, Ed Lewis (tp), Eli Robinson, Jay Jay Johnson, George Matthews, Ted Donnelly (tb), Preston Love, Rudy Rutherford (as), Illinois Jacquet, Buddy Tate (ts), Jack Washington (bs), Count Basie (p), Freddie Green (g), Walter Page (b), Jo Jones (d), Bob Bailey (vcl). *NYC, July 31, 1946*
HOB NAIL BOOGIE (four takes)/DANNY BOY vBB/MUTTON LEG (four takes)/STAY ON IT **(6)**

Harry Edison (tp), Bill Johnson (tb) and Paul Gonzalves (ts) replace Joe Newman, Jay Jay Johnson and Illinois Jacquet. Add Ann Moore, Jimmy Rushing (vcl).

NYC, August 7, 1946

WILD BILL'S BOOGIE (six takes)/FLA-GA-LA-PA vAM/DON'T EVER LET ME BE YOURS vBB/ GOODBYE BABY (three takes) vJR **(6)**

Add Ann Baker (vcl). *NYC, March 13, 1947*
ONE O'CLOCK BOOGIE/MEET ME AT NO SPECIAL PLACE vAB/FUTILE FRUSTRATION **(7)**

COUNT BASIE, HIS INSTRUMENTALISTS AND RHYTHM
Emmett Berry (tp), George Matthews (tb), Charlie Price (as), Paul Gonsalves (ts), Count Basie (p), Freddie Green (g), Walter Page (b), Jo Jones (d)

NYC, May 20, 1947

SWINGIN'THE BLUES –1/ST. LOUIS BOOGIE **(7)**
–1, omit Price

Count Basie (p), Freddie Green (g), Walter Page (b), Jo Jones (d)

NYC, May 21, 1947

SHINE ON HARVEST MOON/SUGAR –1 **(7)**
–1, add Paul Gonsalves (ts)

COUNT BASIE AND HIS ORCHESTRA
Emmett Berry, Ed Lewis, Joe Newman, Harry Edison, Snooky Young (tp), Bill Johnson, George Matthews, Eli Robinson, Ted Donnelly (tb), Charles Price, Preston Love (as), Paul Gonsalves, Buddy Tate (ts), Jack Washington (bs), Count Basie (p), Freddie Green (g), Walter Page (b), Jo Jones (d), Jimmy Rushing (vcl).

NYC, May 23, 1947

AFTER YOU'VE GONE vJR/SOUTH **(7)**

Dicky Wells and George Simon (tb), replace George Matthews and Eli Robinson. Add Bob Bailey (vcl) *Chicago, October 19, 1947*
BLUE AND SENTIMENTAL vBB/SEVENTH AVENUE EXPRESS **(7)**

George Matthews (tb) replaces George Simon. *Hollywood, December 8 & 9, 1947*
SOPHISTICATED SWING/MONEY IS HONEY vJR **(7)**

George Washington (tb) replaces Dicky Wells. *Hollywood, December 12, 1947*
ROBBINS' NEST –1/BYE BYE BABY vJR **(7)**
–1, Basie plays both piano and celeste

Emmett Berry, Harry Edison, Jimmy Nottingham, Clark Terry (tp), Ted Donnelly, Bill Johnson, George Matthews, Dicky Wells (tb), Charles Price, Earl Warren (as), Paul Gonsalves, Wardell Gray (ts). Jack Washington (bs), Count Basie (p), Freddie Green (g), Gene Wright (b), Shadow Wilson (d),. Unknown electric guitar heard on X–1. *Possibly NYC, early/mid September, 1948*
THE KING/SPASMODIC/X–1/GOOD BAIT Spotlite SPJ134

Singleton Palmer (b) probably replaces Gene Wright. *NYC, late 1948*
IT SERVES ME RIGHT/LITTLE DOG Spotlite SPJ134
Note – a second recording ban affected all American gramophone companies throughout the whole of 1948. The above Spotlite LP helps to fill the gap between the 1947 and 1949 RCA Victor sessions.

81

Harry Edison, Emmett Berry, Clark Terry, Jimmy Nottingham, Gerald Wilson (tp), Ted Donnelly, Dicky Wells, George Matthews, Melba Liston (tb), Earl Warren, Charles Price (as), Paul Gonsalves, Bill 'Weasel' Parker (ts), Jack Washington (bs), Count Basie (p), Freddie Green (g), Singleton Palmer (b), Butch Ballard (d), Jimmy Rushing (vcl). *Hollywood, April 11, 1949*
CHEEK TO CHEEK/JUST AN OLD MANUSCRIPT **(7)**

Omit Melba Liston *NYC, June 29, 1949*
SHE'S A WINE-O vJR/SHOUTIN'BLUES **(7)**

NYC, July 13, 1949
ST. LOUIS BABY vJR **(7)**

Add Jimmy Tyler (ts) *NYC, August 5, 1949*
THE SLIDER/NORMANIA **(7)**

COUNT BASIE OCTET
Harry Edison (tp), Dicky Wells (tb), Georgie Auld, Gene Ammons (ts), Count Basie (p), Freddie Green (g), Al McKibbon (b), Gus Johnson (d).
NYC, February 6, 1950
IF YOU SEE MY BABY/RAT RACE/SWEETS **(7)**

Clark Terry (tp), Buddy De Franco (cl), Charlie Rouse (ts), Serge Chaloff (bs), Count Basie (p), Freddy Green (g), Jimmy Lewis (b), Buddy Rich (d)
NYC, May 16, 1950
NEAL'S DEAL (four takes)/BLUEBEARD BLUES (two takes)/GOLDEN BULLET (three takes)/YOU'RE MY BABY YOU (two takes) –1 **(6)**
–1, unknown vocalist added

Wardell Gray (ts), Rudy Rutherford (bs) and Gus Johnson (d) replace Charlie Rouse, Serge Chaloff and Buddy Rich. *NYC, November 2, 1950*
SONG OF THE ISLANDS/THESE FOOLISH THINGS/I'M CONFESSIN'/ONE O'CLOCK JUMP **(6)**

NYC, November 3, 1950
I AIN'T GOT NOBODY/LITTLE WHITE LIES (two takes)/I'LL REMEMBER APRIL/TOOTIE **(6)**

COUNT BASIE AND HIS ORCHESTRA
Al Porcino, Clark Terry, Bob Mitchell, Lamar Wright Jr. (tp), Booty Wood, Leon Comegys. Matthew Gee (tb), Marshall Royal, Rubin Phillips (as), Wardell Gray, Lucky Thompson (ts), Charlie Fowlkes (bs), Count Basie (p), Freddie Green (g), Jimmy Lewis (b), Gus Johnson (d). *NYC, April 10, 1951*
HOWZIT/NAILS/LITTLE PONY/BEAVER JUNCTION **(6)**

Paul Campbell, Joe Newman, Wendell Culley, Charlie Shavers (tp), Henry Coker, Bennie Powell, Jimmy Wilkins (tb), Marshall Royal, Ernie Wilkins (as), Floyd 'Candy' Johnson, Paul Quinichette (ts), Charlie Fowlkes (bs), Count Basie (p), Freddie Green (g), Jimmy Lewis (b), Gus Johnson (d). *NYC, January 19, 1952*
NEW BASIE BLUES/SURE THING/WHY NOT?/FAWNCY MEETING YOU
Verve (Eu) 2317074

JIVE AT FIVE –1/NO NAME/REDHEAD/EVERY TUB   Verve (Eu) 2317074
Note – above four titles also on Verve (Eu) 2304 410
–1, Four tp, Henry Coker (tb), Paul Quinichette (ts), same p, g, b, d.

PAUL QUINICHETTE AND HIS ORCHESTRA
Buck Clayton (tp), Dicky Wells (tb), Paul Quinichette (ts), Count Basie (p), Freddie
Green (g), Walter Page (b), Gus Johnson (d).   *NYC, circa March, 1952*
SHAD ROE/PAUL'S BUNION/CREW CUT/THE HOOK/SAMIE –1/I'LL ALWAYS BE IN LOVE
WITH YOU –1   Trip 5542
–1, omit Clayton and Wells. Basie plays organ.

COUNT BASIE AND HIS ORCHESTRA
Personnel as for January 17, 1953 but Reunald Jones (tp) and Eddie 'Lockjaw' Davis
(ts) replace Charlie Shavers and Floyd Johnson   *NYC, July 22 to 26, 1952*
JACK AND JILL/BREAD/THERE'S A SMALL HOTEL/HOB NAIL BOOGIE/BASIE TALKS/
PARADISE SQUAT/BUNNY/TIPPIN'ON THE QT   Verve (Eu) 2317074
Note – Verve (Eu) 2304 410 contains BREAD, THERE'S A SMALL HOTEL AND TIPPIN' ON
THE QT plus BLEE BLOP BLUES which is from the same session.

Same location and date as last but Oscar Peterson (p) and Ray Brown (b) replace Basie
and Jimmy Lewis.
BE MY GUEST   Verve (Eu) 2304 410

Same date but personnel comprises Eddie 'Lockjaw' Davis, Paul Quinichette (ts),
Count Basie (org), Oscar Peterson (p), Freddie Green (g), Ray Brown (b), Gus Johnson
(d) only.
BLUES FOR THE COUNT AND OSCAR   Verve (Eu) 2304 410

Full band personnel as for July 22 to 26, 1952 but Gene Ramey (b) replaces Jimmy
Lewis. Add Al Hibbler (vcl).   *NYC, December 12, 1952*
SENT FOR YOU YESTERDAY vAH/GOIN' TO CHICAGO vAH   Verve (Eu) 2304 410

COUNT BASIE NONET/SEXTET/QUINTET
Wendell Culley (tp), Henry Coker (tb), Marshall Royal (cl), Paul Quinichette (ts),
Charlie Fowlkes (bs), Count Basie (p, org), Freddie Green (g), Gene Ramey (b), Buddy
Rich (d).   *NYC, December 12 and 13, 1952*
I WANT A LITTLE GIRL   Verve MGV8090

Joe Newman (tp) replaces Culley. Omit Henry Coker, Marshall Royal and Charlie
Fowlkes.   *Same dates.*
LADY BE GOOD/BASIE BEAT/SHE'S FUNNY THAT WAY/COUNT'S ORGAN BLUES/KC
ORGAN BLUES/STAN SHORTHAIR/AS LONG AS I LIVE/ROYAL GARDEN BLUES/BLUE AND
SENTIMENTAL –1/SONG OF THE ISLANDS –1   Verve MGV8090
–1, omit Joe Newman

COUNT BASIE AND HIS ORCHESTRA

Joe Wilder, Reunald Jones, Wendell Culley, Joe Newman (tp), Henderson Chambers, Henry Coker, Benny Powell (tb), Marshall Royal (cl, as), Ernie Wilkins (as, ts), Frank Wess (ts, f), Frank Foster (ts), Charlie Fowlkes (bs), Count Basie (p), Freddie Green (g), Eddie Jones (b), Gus Johnson (d) *NYC, December 12, 1953*
STRAIGHT LIFE/BASIE GOES WESS/SOFTLY WITH FEELING/CHERRY POINT/BUBBLES/
RIGHT ON/BLUES DONE COME BACK/PEACE PIPE Verve 2–2517

Thad Jones (tp) replaces Joe Wilder *NYC, August 16-17, 1954*
STEREOPHONIC/MAMBO MIST/SIXTEEN MEN SWINGING/SHE'S JUST MY SIZE/I FEEL LIKE A NEW MAN/YOU FOR ME/SOFT DRINK/TWO FOR THE BLUES/SLOW BUT SURE/
BLUES BACKSTAGE/DOWN FOR THE COUNT/PERDIDO/TWO FRANKS/SKA-DI-DLE-DEE-
BEE-DOO/RAILS/EVENTIDE/AIN'T MISBEHAVIN' Verve 2–2517

JOE NEWMAN AND THE BOYS IN THE BAND (original title on Storyville release)

COUNT BASIE – AIN'T IT THE TRUTH (reissue title on Black Lion)

Joe Newman (tp), Henry Coker (tb), Frank Wess (ts, f), Charlie Fowlkes (bs), Count Basie (p, org), Freddie Green (g), Eddie Jones (b), Gus Johnson (d) *Boston, September 7, 1954*
IN CASE YOU DIDN'T KNOW (two takes)/THESE FOOLISH THINGS (two takes)/PETER PAN/AIN'T IT THE TRUTH/INGIN' THE OOH/CONFESSIN' Black Lion (Eu) BLM51009

COUNT BASIE AND HIS ORCHESTRA – APRIL IN PARIS

Wendell Culley, Reunald Jones, Thad Jones, Joe Newman (tp), Henry Coker, Bill Hughes, Benny Powell (tb), Marshall Royal (cl, as), Bill Graham (as), Frank Wess (ts, f), Frank Foster (ts), Charlie Fowlkes (bs), Count Basie (p), Freddie Green (g), Eddie Jones (b), Sonny Payne (d). *NYC, July 26, 1955*
APRIL IN PARIS/CORNER POCKET/DIDN'T YOU?/SWEETIE CAKES Verve MGV8012

 NYC, January 4, 1956
MAGIC/SHINY STOCKINGS/WHAT AM I HERE FOR?/MIDGETS Verve MGV8012

Add Quincy Jones (tp) *NYC, January 5, 1956*
MAMBO INN –1/DINNER WITH FRIENDS Verve MGV8012
–1, add Jose Mangual (bongo) and Ubaldo Nieto (timbales)

COUNT BASIE AND HIS ORCHESTRA – BASIE IN LONDON (sic)

Omit Quincy Jones. Add Joe Williams (vcl).
 Concert, Gothenberg, Sweden, September 7, 1956
JUMPIN'AT THE WOODSIDE/SHINY STOCKINGS/HOW HIGH THE MOON/FLUTE JUICE/
NAILS/BLEE BLOP BLUES/ALRIGHT, OK, YOU WIN vJW/ROLL 'EM PETE vJW/THE COMEBACK vJW/BLUES BACKSTAGE/CORNER POCKET/ONE O'CLOCK JUMP Verve MGV8199

COUNT BASIE AT NEWPORT

Same personnel. *Newport Jazz Festival, July 7, 1957*
SWINGIN'AT NEWPORT Verve MGV8243

Add Lester Young (ts) and Jimmy Rushing (vcl). Jo Jones (d) replaces Sonny Payne. *Same concert*

POLKA DOTS AND MOONBEAMS/LESTER LEAPS IN/SENT FOR YOU YESTERDAY vJR/ BOOGIE WOOGIE vJR/EVENIN' vJR/ONE O'CLOCK JUMP –1

–1, add Roy Eldridge (tp) and Illinois Jacquet (ts)   Verve MGV8243

THE ATOMIC MISTER BASIE
Joe Newman, Thad Jones, Wendell Culley, Snooky Young (tp), Benny Powell, Henry Coker, Al Grey (tb), Marshall Royal (cl, as), Frank Wess (as, f), Frank Foster, Eddie 'Lockjaw' Davis (ts), Charlie Fowlkes (bs), Count Basie (p), Freddie Green (g), Eddie Jones (b), Sonny Payne (d), Neal Hefti (arr).   *NYC, October 21 & 22, 1957*

THE KID FROM RED BANK/DUET/AFTER SUPPER/FLIGHT OF THE FOO BIRDS/DOUBLE-O/TEDDY THE TOAD/WHIRLY-BIRD/MIDNITE BLUE/SPLANKY/FANTAIL/LI'L DARLIN'
                                                                      Roulette R52003

Note – the above details refer to the original issues of this LP. Some (but not all) later reissues omitted certain titles.

COUNT BASIE ALL STARS
Emmett Berry, Doc Cheatham, Roy Eldridge, Joe Newman (tp), Vic Dickenson, Frank Rehak, Dicky Wells (tb), Earl Warren (as), Lester Young, Coleman Hawkins (ts), Harry Carney (bs), Count Basie (p), Freddie Green (g), Eddie Jones (b), Jo Jones (d), Jimmy Rushing (vcl).   *NYC, December 4, 1957*

DICKIE'S DREAM/I LEFT MY BABY vJR   Columbia JCL1098

BASIE PLAYS HEFTI
Personnel as for October 21 & 22, 1957 except Billy Mitchell (ts) replaces Eddie Davis. Neal Hefti (arr).   *NYC, April 3, 4 & 14, 1958*

HAS ANYONE HERE SEEN BASIE?/CUTE/PENSIVE MISS/SLOO FOOT/IT'S AWFULLY NICE TO BE WITH YOU/SCOOT/A LITTLE TEMPO PLEASE/LATE DATE/COUNTDOWN/BAG-A-BONES/PONY TAIL   Roulette R52011

BASIE – ONE MORE TIME
Personnel as last but Quincy Jones (arr) replaces Hefti   *NYC, December 18 to 20, 1958 and NYC, January 23 & 24, 1959*

FOR LENA AND LENNIE/RAT RACE/QUINCE/JESSICA'S DAY/THE BIG WALK/A SQUARE AT THE ROUND TABLE/I NEEDS TO BE BEE'D WITH/MEET BB/THE MIDNIGHT SUN NEVER SETS/MUTTNIK   Roulette R52024

BASIE – CHAIRMAN OF THE BOARD
Personnel as last but Frank Foster, Frank Wess, Thad Jones and Ernie Wilkins (arr) replace Quincy Jones and Mundell Lowe (g) replaces Green.
                                    -          *NYC, April 28 & 29, 1959*

BLUES IN HOSS'S FLAT/HRH (HER ROYAL HIGHNESS)/SEGUE IN C/KANSAS CITY SHOUT/ SPEAKING OF SOUNDS/TV TIME/WHO, ME?/THE DEACON/HALF MOON STREET/MUTT AND JEFF   Roulette R52032

THE COUNT BASIE STORY
Personnel as for October 21 & 22, 1957 except Sonny Cohen (tp) replaces Wendell Culley. Omit Neal Hefti and add Joe Williams (vcl). *NYC, June, July, 1960*
DOWN FOR DOUBLE/LESTER LEAPS IN/TOPSY/AVENUE C/JUMPIN' AT THE WOODSIDE/ TAPS MILLER/SHORTY GEORGE/DOGGIN' AROUND/ROCK-A-BYE-BASIE/RED BANK BOOGIE/OUT THE WINDOW/SWINGIN' THE BLUES/BLUE AND SENTIMENTAL/EVERY TUB/TICKLE TOE/DICKIE'S DREAM/TEXAS SHUFFLE/9.20 SPECIAL/BROADWAY –1/SENT FOR YOU YESTERDAY vJW –1/BOOGIE WOOGIE vJW –1/JIVE AT FIVE –2/TIME OUT –2   Roulette RB–1
Note – Roulette RB–1 is a two-LP set. –1, Gus Johnson (d) replaces Sonny Payne on these tracks. –2, Jimmy Nottingham (tp) and Seldon Powell (ts) replace Thad Jones and Frank Foster on these tracks.

COUNT BASIE – NOT NOW, I'LL TELL YOU WHEN
Personnel as for DOWN FOR DOUBLE on previous album.   *NYC, July 15, 1960*
NOT NOW I'LL TELL YOU WHEN/RARE BUTTERFLY/BACK TO THE APPLE/OL'MAN RIVER/ MAMA'S TALKIN' SOFT/THE DAILY JUMP/BLUE ON BLUE/SWINGING AT THE WALDORF/ SWEET AND PRETTY   Roulette R52044

COUNT BASIE – KANSAS CITY SUITE
Same but add Benny Carter (arr)   *NYC, November 17, 1960*
VINE STREET RUMBLE/KATY DO/MISS MISSOURI/JACKSON COUNTY JUBILEE/SUNSET GLOW/MEETIN' TIME/PASEO PROMENADE/BLUE FIVE JIVE/ROMPIN' AT THE RENO/THE WIGGLE WALK   Roulette R52056

COUNT BASIE – EASIN' IT
Personnel as for July 15, 1960 plus Clark Terry (tp).   *NYC, late 1960*
EASIN' IT/BROTHERLY SHOVE/BLUES FOR DADDY-O   Roulette R52106

Thad Jones, Fip Ricard, Sonny Cohen, Al Aarons (tp), Henry Coker, Quentin Jackson, Benny Powell (tb), Marshall Royal (cl, as), Frank Wess (as, ts, f), Frank Foster (ts), Eric Dixon (f, ts), Charlie Fowlkes (bs), Count Basie (p), Freddie Green (g), Art Davis (b), Gus Johnson (d)   *NYC, July 3, 13 and 26, 1962*
FOUR-FIVE-SIX/IT'S ABOUT TIME –1/MISUNDERSTOOD BLUES –2/MAMA DEV –2
–1, Ike Isaacs (b) for Davis; –2,Louie Bellson (d) for Johnson   Roulette R52106
Note – all compositions and arrangements on this LP by Frank Foster.

COUNT BASIE AND HIS ORCHESTRA – AT BIRDLAND
Sonny Cohen, Lennie Johnson, Thad Jones, Snooky Young (tp), Henry Coker, Quentin Jackson, Benny Powell (tb), Marshall Royal (cl, as), Frank Wess (as, ts, f), Frank Foster, Budd Johnson (ts), Charlie Fowlkes (bs), Count Basie (p), Freddie Green (g), Eddie Jones (b), Sonny Payne (d), Jon Hendricks (vcl).
Birdland club, NYC, July 28, 1961
LITTLE PONY/WHIRLY BIRD vJH/ONE O'CLOCK JUMP (short version)/DISCOMMOTION/ BLUES BACKSTAGE/BLEE BLOP BLUES/SEGUE IN C/GOOD TIME BLUES/ONE O'CLOCK JUMP (long version)   Roulette R52065

COUNT BASIE – THE LEGEND

As previous personnel but Al Aarons (tp) and Sam Herman (g) replace Lennie Johnson and Freddie Green. Add Benny Carter (as, arr). Omit Jon Hendricks and Marshall Royal. *NYC, October 30 & 31, 1961*
and NYC, November 1 & 2, 1961

THE TROT/THE LEGEND/GOIN'ON/EASY MONEY/WHO'S BLUE?/AMOROSO/THE SWIZZLE/
TURNABOUT Roulette R52086

COUNT BASIE AND HIS KANSAS CITY SEVEN

Thad Jones (tp), Eric Dixon, Frank Wess (f, ts), Count Basie (p, org), Freddie Green (g), Eddie Jones (b), Sonny Payne (d) *NYC, March 21, 1962*
SECRETS/SENATOR WHITEHEAD/WHAT'CHA TALKIN'? Impulse A 15

Frank Foster (ts) replaces Frank Wess *NYC, March 22, 1962*
OH, LADY BE GOOD/I WANT A LITTLE GIRL/SHOE SHINE BOY/COUNT'S PLACE/TALLY-
HO, MR BASIE Impulse A 15

COUNT BASIE – IN SWEDEN

Thad Jones, Sonny Cohen, Fip Ricard, Al Aarons (tp), Benny Powell, Quentin Jackson, Henry Coker (tb), Marshall Royal (cl, as), Frank Wess (as, ts, f), Eric Dixon (f, ts), Frank Foster (ts), Charlie Fowlkes (bs), Count Basie (p), Freddie Green (g), Ike Isaacs (b), Louie Bellson (d) *Concert, Stockholm, August 11 & 12, 1962*
PLYMOUTH ROCK –1/GOOD TIME BLUES –1/BLUES BACKSTAGE –1/LITTLE PONY –1, 2/
WHO, ME? –1, 2/PEACE PIPE/APRIL IN PARIS/BACKWATER BLUES –3 Roulette R52099
–1, add Ake Persson (tb), –2, add Benny Bailey (tp), –3, add Irene Reid (vcl)

COUNT BASIE – ON MY WAY AND SHOUTIN' AGAIN

Ernie Royal, Fip Ricard, Thad Jones, Sonny Cohen, Al Aarons (tp), Grover Mitchell, Henry Coker, Benny Powell (tb), Marshall Royal (cl, as), Frank Wess (as, ts, f), Eric Dixon (f, ts), Frank Foster (ts), Charlie Fowlkes (bs), Count Basie (p), Freddie Green (g), Buddy Catlett (b), Sonny Payne (d), Neal Hefti (arr) *NYC, November 2, 3 & 5, 1962*
ROSE BUD/DUCKY BUMPS/THE LONG NIGHT/JUMP FOR JOHNNY/TOGETHER AGAIN/
AIN'T THAT RIGHT?/SHANGHAIED/SKIPPIN' WITH SKITCH/EEE DEE/I'M SHOUTING AGAIN
Verve MGV 8511

COUNT BASIE – LI'L OL' GROOVEMAKER

Snooky Young, Al Aarons, Sonny Cohen, Don Rader, Fip Ricard (tp), Henry Coker, Grover Mitchell, Benny Powell, Urbie Green (tb), Marshall Royal (as, cl), Eric Dixon (f, ts), Frank Wess (as, ts, f), Frank Foster (ts), Charlie Fowlkes (bs), Count Basie (p), Freddie Green (g), Buddy Catlett (b), Sonny Payne (d), Quincy Jones (arr).
NYC, April 21, 22 & 23, 1963
LI'L OL' GROOVEMAKER. . .BASIE/PLEASINGLY PLUMP/BOODY RUMBLE/BELLY ROLL/
COUNT 'EM/NASTY MAGNUS/DUM DUM/LULLABY FOR JOLIE/KANSAS CITY WRINKLES
Verve MGV 8549

COUNT BASIE AND HIS ORCHESTRA – BASIE-LAND

As previous personnel but Billy Byers (arr) replaces Quincy Jones *NYC, April, 1963*
BASIE-LAND/BIG BROTHER/COUNT ME IN/WANDERLUST/INSTANT BLUES/RABBLE ROUSER/
SASSY/GYMNASTICS/YURIKO/DOODLE-OODLE Verve MGV 8597

COUNT BASIE – BASIE'S BEAT

Al Aarons, Sonny Cohen, Wallace Davenport, Phil Gilbeau (tp), Grover Mitchell, Henderson Chambers, Bill Hughes, Al Grey (tb), Marshall Royal (cl, as), Bobby Plater (as, f), Eric Dixon (f, ts), Eddie 'Lockjaw' Davis (ts), Charlie Fowlkes (bs), Count Basie (p), Freddie Green (g), Norman Keenan (b), Rufus Jones (d)

NYC, October 7, 8 & 9, 1965
IT'S ONLY A PAPER MOON/ST. LOUIS BLUES/HEY JIM/HAPPY HOUSE/MAKIN' WHOOPEE
Verve MGV 8687

Al Aarons, Sonny Cohen, Gene Goe, Harry Edison (tp), Grover Mitchell, Richard Boone, Harlan Floyd (tb), Bill Hughes (b-tb), Marshall Royal (cl, as), Bobby Plater (as), Eric Dixon (f, ts), Billy Mitchell (ts), Charlie Fowlkes (bs), Count Basie (p), Freddie Green (g), Norman Keenan (b), Ed Shaughnessy (d)   *NYC, February 15, 1967*
SQUEEZE ME/I GOT RHYTHM –1/FRANKIE AND JOHNNY/BOONE'S BLUES –1
–1, Richard Boone (vcl) on these titles   Verve MGV 8687

COUNT BASIE – THE GREAT CONCERT

Al Aarons, Sonny Cohen, Wallace Davenport, Phil Gilbeau (tp), Grover Mitchell, Henderson Chambers, Al Grey (tb), Richard Boone (tb, vcl), Marshall Royal (cl, as), Bobby Plater (f, as), Eric Dixon (f, ts), Eddie 'Lockjaw' Davis (ts), Charlie Fowlkes (bs), Count Basie (p), Freddie Green (g), Al Lucas (b), Rufus Jones (d), unidentified female vocalist on –1.   *Unknown US location, July 23 or 24, 1968*
ALL OF ME/FLIGHT OF THE FOO BIRDS/BOONE BLUES vRB/STORMY MONDAY BLUES –1/ THE MAGIC FLEA/WEE BABY BLUES –1/IN A MELLOW TONE/WHIRLY BIRD/NIGHT IN TUNISIA/HITTIN' TWELVE/CHEROKEE/THE MIDNIGHT SUN WILL NEVER SET/BLUES FOR EILEEN/JUMPIN' AT THE WOODSIDE/APRIL IN PARIS/I GOT RHYTHM vRB/I NEEDS TO BE BEE'D WITH/LI'L DARLIN'/ALL HEART/ONE O'CLOCK JUMP

Festival Album (F) 231
Note – the personnel, location and date printed on the sleeve of the Festival album are incorrect.

COUNT BASIE – STRAIGHT AHEAD

Gene Goe, Sonny Cohen, Oscar Brashear, Al Aarons (tp), Grover Mitchell, Richard Boone, Bill Hughes, Steve Galloway (tb), Marshall Royal (cl, as) Bobby Plater (f, as), Eric Dixon (f, ts), Eddie 'Lockjaw' Davis (ts), Charlie Fowlkes (bs), Count Basie (p), Freddie Green (g), Norman Keenan (b), Harold Jones (d), Sammy Nestico (arr)

Hollywood, August 31, September 3 & 4, 1968
BASIE-STRAIGHT AHEAD/IT'S SO NICE/LONELY STREET/FUN TIME/MAGIC FLEA/SWITCH IN TIME/HAY BURNER/THAT WARM FEELING –1/THE QUEEN BEE
–1, add Sammy Nestico (p); Basie plays organ on this track.   Dot 25902

COUNT BASIE – STANDING OVATION

As previous personnel but Frank Hooks (tb), replaces Steve Galloway. Add Harry Edison (tp).   *Tropicana Hotel, Las Vegas, c. March, 1969*
DOWN FOR DOUBLE/LI'L DARLIN'/BROADWAY/JIVE AT FIVE/CHERRY POINT/JUMPIN' AT THE WOODSIDE/ONE O'CLOCK JUMP/SHINY STOCKINGS/BLUE AND SENTIMENTAL/ EVERY TUB/CORNER POCKET/THE KID FROM RED BANK/ONE O'CLOCK JUMP

Dot 25938

COUNT BASIE AND HIS ORCHESTRA – AFRIQUE
Paul Cohen, Sonny Cohen, Pete Minger, Waymon Reed (tp), Steve Galloway, Mel Wanzo, John Watson Sr., Bill Hughes (tb), Bobby Plater (f, as), Bill Adkins (as), Eric Dixon (f, ts), Eddie 'Lockjaw' Davis (ts), Cecil Payne (bs), Hubert Laws (f), Count Basie (p), Freddie Green (g), John B. Williams (elec b), Harold Jones (d), Richard Landrum (conga), Sonny Morgan (bongos), Oliver Nelson (arr)
NYC, December 22, 1970

KILIMANJARO/HOBO FLATS –1/GYPSY QUEEN/AFRICAN SUNRISE
–1, add Buddy Lucas (harmonica)   RCA (F) PL 43547

Personnel as previous session but Bob Aston (ts) replaces Eddie 'Lockjaw' Davis
NYC, December 23, 1970

STEP RIGHT UP –1, 2/AFRIQUE –3/LOVE FLOWER –1/JAPAN
–1, add Oliver Nelson (as); –2, Norman Keenan (b) replaces John B. Williams on this title; –3, add Warren Smith (marimba)   RCA (F) PL 43547

COUNT BASIE – HAVE A NICE DAY
Paul Cohen, Sonny Cohen, Pete Minger, Waymon Reed (tp), Al Grey, Bill Hughes, Grover Mitchell, Mel Wanzo, John Watson Sr. (tb), Curtis Peagler (as), Bobby Plater (f, as), Eric Dixon (f, ts), Eddie 'Lockjaw' Davis (ts), J. C. Williams (bs), Count Basie (p), Freddie Green (g), Norman Keenan (b), Harold Jones (d), Sammy Nestico (arr)   *Hollywood, July–August, 1971*
HAVE A NICE DAY/THE PLUNGER/JAMIE/IT'S ABOUT TIME/THIS WAY/SCOTT'S PLACE/ DOIN' BASIE'S THING/THE SPIRIT IS WILLING/SMALL TALK/YOU'N ME/FEELIN' FREE
Daybreak 2005

COUNT BASIE – BASIE JAM
Harry Edison (tp), Jay Jay Johnson (tb), Zoot Sims, Eddie 'Lockjaw' Davis (ts), Count Basie (p, org), Irving Ashby (g), Ray Brown (b), Louie Bellson (d)
Hollywood, December 10, 1973
DOUBLING BLUES/HANGING OUT/REDBANK BLUES/ONE-NIGHTER/FREEPORT BLUES
Pablo 2310 718

JOE TURNER–COUNT BASIE – THE BOSSES
Personnel as last session plus Joe Turner (vcl)   *Hollywood, December 11, 1973*
HONEYDRIPPER/HONEY HUSH/CHERRY RED/NIGHT TIME IS THE RIGHT TIME/BLUES AROUND THE CLOCK/SINCE I FELL FOR YOU/FLIP, FLOP & FLY/WEE BABY BLUES/GOOD MORNIN' BLUES/ROLL 'EM PETE   Pablo 2310 709

COUNT BASIE TRIO – FOR THE FIRST TIME
Count Basie (p, org –1), Ray Brown (b), Louie Bellson (d).   *Hollywood, May 22, 1974*
BABY LAWRENCE/PRES/I'LL ALWAYS BE IN LOVE WITH YOU/BLUES IN CHURCH –1/LADY BE GOOD (Concept 1)/LADY BE GOOD (Concept 2)/BLUES IN THE ALLEY/AS LONG AS I LIVE/SONG OF THE ISLANDS –1/ROYAL GARDEN BLUES/(UN)EASY DOES IT/OP
Pablo 2310 712

OSCAR PETERSON AND COUNT BASIE – SATCH AND JOSH
Count Basie (p, org), Oscar Peterson (p), Freddie Green (g), Ray Brown (b), Louie Bellson (d)   *Hollywood, December 2, 1974*
BUNS BLUES/THESE FOOLISH THINGS/'RB'/BURNING/EXACTLY LIKE YOU/JUMPIN' AT THE WOODSIDE/LOUIE B/LESTER LEAPS IN/BIG STOCKINGS/S & J BLUES
Pablo 2310 722

BASIE & ZOOT
Zoot Sims (ts), Count Basie (p, org), John Heard (b), Louie Bellson (d)

NYC, April 9, 1975

I NEVER KNEW/IT'S ONLY A PAPER MOON/BLUES FOR NAT COLE/CAPTAIN BLIGH/
HONEYSUCKLE ROSE/HARDAY/MEAN TO ME/I SURRENDER DEAR   Pablo 2310 745

COUNT BASIE AND HIS ORCHESTRA – BASIE BIG BAND
Pete Minger, Frank Szabo, Dave Stahl, Bobby Mitchell, Sonny Cohn (tp), Al Grey,
Curtis Fuller, Bill Hughes, Mel Wanzo (tb), Danny Turner (as), Bobby Plater (f, as),
Eric Dixon (f, ts), Jimmy Forrest (ts), Charlie Fowlkes (bs), Count Basie (p), Freddie
Green (g), John Duke (b), Butch Miles (d), Sammy Nestico (arr)

Hollywood, August 26 & 27, 1975

FRONT BURNER/FRECKLE FACE/ORANGE SHERBET/SOFT AS VELVET/THE HEAT'S ON/
MIDNIGHT FREIGHT/GIVE 'M TIME/THE WIND MACHINE/TALL COTTON

Pablo 2310 756

COUNT BASIE KANSAS CITY 3 – FOR THE SECOND TIME
Count Basie (p), Ray Brown (b), Louie Bellson (d).   *Hollywood, August 28, 1975*
SANDMAN/IF I COULD BE WITH YOU ONE HOUR TONIGHT/DRAW/ON THE SUNNY SIDE
OF THE STREET/THE ONE I LOVE BELONGS TO SOMEBODY ELSE/BLUES FOR ERIC/I
SURRENDER DEAR/RACEHORSE   Pablo 2310 878

COUNT BASIE AND HIS ORCHESTRA – I TOLD YOU SO
Sonny Cohn, Pete Minger, Bobby Mitchell, John Thomas, Jack Feierman (tp), Al
Grey, Curtis Fuller, Bill Hughes, Mel Wanzo (tb), Danny Turner (as), Bobby Plater
(f, as), Eric Dixon (f, ts), Jimmy Forrest (ts), Charlie Fowlkes (bs), Count Basie (p),
Freddie Green (g), John Duke (b), Butch Miles (d), Bill Holman (arr).

NYC, January 12, 13 & 14, 1976

TREE FROG/FLIRT/BLUES FOR ALFY/SOMETHING TO LIVE FOR/PLAIN BROWN WRAPPER/
SWEE'PEA/TICKER/TOO CLOSE FOR COMFORT/TOLD YOU SO/THE GIT

Pablo 2310 767

HARRY EDISON – EDISON'S LIGHTS
Harry Edison (tp), Eddie 'Lockjaw' Davis (ts), Count Basie (p), John Heard (d), Jimmy
Smith (d).   *Hollywood, May 5, 1976*
EDISON'S LIGHTS/AIN'T MISBEHAVIN'/AVALON/'E'   Pablo 2310 780

BASIE JAM No. 2
Clark Terry (tp), Al Grey (tb), Benny Carter (as), Eddie 'Lockjaw' Davis (ts), Count
Basie (p), Joe Pass (g), John Heard (b), Louie Bellson (d)

Hollywood, May 6, 1976

MAMA DON'T WEAR NO DRAWERS/DOGGIN' AROUND/KANSAS CITY LINE/JJJJUMP
Pablo 2335 748

BASIE JAM No. 3
Personnel and date as last session.
BYE BYE BLUES/MOTEN SWING/I SURRENDER DEAR/SONG OF THE ISLANDS

Pablo 2310 840

COUNT BASIE AND HIS ORCHESTRA – PRIME TIME

Personnel as for January, 1976 but Lyn Biviano (tp) replaces John Thomas and Jack Feierman. Sammy Nestico (arr) replaces Bill Holman

Hollywood, January 18, 19 & 20, 1977

PRIME TIME/BUNDLE O' FUNK –1/SWEET GEORGIA BROWN/FEATHERWEIGHT/REACHIN'
OUT/JA–DA/THE GREAT DEBATE/YA GOTTA TRY –2   Pablo 2310 797

–1, add Reinie Press (Fender bass); –2, Nat Pierce (p) replaces Count Basie.

COUNT BASIE AND DIZZY GILLESPIE – THE GIFTED ONES

Dizzy Gillespie (tp), Count Basie (p), Ray Brown (b), Mickey Roker (d)

Las Vegas, February 3, 1977

BACK TO THE LAND/CONSTANTINOPLE/YOU GOT IT/ST. JAMES INFIRMARY/FOLLOW
THE LEADER/OW   Pablo 2310 833

COUNT BASIE JAM

Roy Eldridge (tp), Vic Dickenson, Al Grey (tb), Benny Carter (as), Zoot Sims (ts), Count Basie (p), Ray Brown (b), Jimmy Smith (d).

Jazz Festival, Montreux, July 14, 1977

BOOKIE BLUES/SHE'S FUNNY THAT WAY/THESE FOOLISH THINGS/KIDNEY STEW/TRIO
BLUES/I GOT IT BAD/JUMPIN' AT THE WOODSIDE   Pablo 2308 209

COUNT BASIE BIG BAND – MONTREUX '77

Waymon Reed, Lyn Biviano, Sonny Cohn, Bobby Mitchell (tp), Al Grey, Dennis Wilson, Mel Wanzo, Bill Hughes (tb), Danny Turner (as), Bobby Plater (f, as), Eric Dixon (f, ts), Jimmy Forrest (ts), Charlie Fowlkes (bs), Count Basie (p); Freddie Green (g), John Duke (b), Butch Miles (d).   *Jazz Festival, Montreux, July 15, 1977*

THE HEAT'S ON/FRECKLE FACE/SPLANKY/THE MORE I SEE YOU/NIGHT IN TUNISIA/
HITTIN' 12/BAG OF DREAMS/THINGS AIN'T WHAT THEY USED TO BE/I NEEDS TO BE
BEE'D WITH/LI'L DARLIN'/JUMPIN' AT THE WOODSIDE/ONE O'CLOCK JUMP

Pablo 2308 207

OSCAR PETERSON AND COUNT BASIE – SATCH AND JOSH. . .AGAIN

Oscar Peterson (p), Count Basie (p), John Heard (b), Louie Bellson (d)

Hollywood, September 20, 1977

ROOTS/RED WAGON/HOME RUN/SWEETHEARTS ON PARADE/LI'L DARLIN' –1/THE TIME
IS RIGHT/CHERRY/LESTER LEAPS IN/SHE'S FUNNY THAT WAY/LADY FITZ –2

Pablo 2310 802

–1, Peterson (electric piano on this track); –2, Count Basie (electric piano on this track)

COUNT BASIE & OSCAR PETERSON – NIGHT RIDER

Count Basie (p, org –1), Oscar Peterson (p, elec-p –2), John Heard (b), Louie Bellson (d)   *Hollywood, February 21 & 22, 1978*

NIGHT RIDER/MEMORIES OF YOU –1/9.20 SPECIAL/SWEET LORRAINE/IT'S A WONDERFUL
WORLD/BLUES FOR PAMELA –2   Pablo 2310 843

COUNT BASIE AND HIS ORCHESTRA – ON THE ROAD

Pete Minger, Sonny Cohn, Paul Cohen, Ray Brown (tp), Booty Wood, Bill Hughes, Mel Wanzo, Dennis Wilson (tb), Danny Turner (as), Bobby Plater (f, as), Eric Dixon (f, ts), Kenny Hing (ts), Charlie Fowlkes (bs), Count Basie (p), Freddie Green (g), John Clayton (b), Butch Miles (d), Dennis Roland (vcl).

Jazz Festival, Montreux, July 12, 1979

WIND MACHINE/BLUES FOR STEPHANIE/JOHN THE III/THERE WILL NEVER BE ANOTHER YOU/BOOTIE'S BLUES/SPLANKY/BASIE/WATCH WHAT HAPPENS vDR/WORK SONG vDR/ IN A MELLOW TONE   Pablo 2312 112

COUNT BASIE SIX – KANSAS CITY

Willie Cook (tp), Eddie 'Cleanhead' Vinson (as, vcl), Count Basie (p), Joe Pass (g), Niels Henning Orsted Pedersen (b), Louie Bellson (d)   *Las Vegas, November 1, 1981*

WALKING THE BLUES/BLUES FOR LITTLE JAZZ/VEGAS DRAG/WEE BABY vEV/SCOOTER/ ST. LOUIS BLUES/OPUS SIX   Pablo 2310 871

Index to Discography

I know from past experience that it is impossible to keep abreast of the record market when compiling a reference book. I have therefore listed what I believe are the most recent, or most useful, catalogue numbers knowing that by the time this book appears in print the wholesale reissue of Count Basie material will have overtaken me. From 1955 onwards I have given the best-known album titles as these have usually been retained in recycling exercises; I think it is probably more useful to know that an LP is called 'Not Now I'll Tell You When' than to try to find the most recent catalogue number. Fortunately the majority of Basie's records from 1936 to 1951 are contained in a series of albums ranging from a two-LP set on RCA to two ten-LP sets covering Basie's entire Columbia output, compiled by my good friend Henri Renaud. Although these albums are all of French origin there should be no difficulty in obtaining them via the specialist shops. Any other issued compilations of MCA or Columbia material pale into insignificance alongside the issues listed here. To save space I have allocated code reference numbers to such compendia releases and list them below. Other abbreviations to note are 'Eu' for a European release and 'F' for French. All Roulette catalogue numbers are those of the first issues of this material. Some of the broadcast albums on labels such as Jazz Archives etc. may be difficult to obtain but they have been included here because of their extreme historical and musical value.

KEY TO CODE NUMBERS:

(1) *The Complete Count Basie, Vols. 1 to 10,* CBS(F) 66101 (ten LPs)

(2) *Count Basie – Complete Recorded Works In Chronological Order, 1937 to 1939,* MCA(F) 510.167/510.170 (four LPs)

(3) *Count Basie At The Chatterbox* – Jazz Archives JA-16

(4) *Spirituals To Swing Concert,* Vanguard, reissued as Vogue (E) VJD550 (two LPs)

(5) *Count Basie And His Orchestra,* Jazz Society (Eu) AA-512

(6) *The Complete Count Basie, Vols. 11 to 20,* CBS(F) 66102 (ten LPs)

(7) *Count Basie, Masters Of Jazz,* RCA(F) CL42113 (two LPs)

Bibliography

The following works have been of inestimable value to me in the preparation of this book:

Allen, Walter C: *Hendersonia*. Highland Park, NJ, Jazz Monographs No.4

Chilton, John: *Who's Who Of Jazz*. London, Bloomsbury Bookshop

Dance, Stanley: *The World of Count Basie*. London, Sidgwick & Jackson; New York, Charles Scribner's Sons

Feather, Leonard: *From Satchmo to Miles*. New York, Stein and Day; London, Quartet.

Feather, Leonard: *The Encyclopedia of Jazz, Encyclopedia of Jazz in the Sixties* and *Encyclopedia of Jazz in the Seventies*. New York, Bonanza Books; London, Quartet.

Hammond, John: *John Hammond On Record*. USA, Ridge Press; London, Penguin.

Hentoff, Nat: *The Jazz Life*. London, Panther Books.

Horricks, Raymond: *Count Basie And His Orchestra*. London, Victor Gollancz.

Shapiro, Nat and Hentoff, Nat: *Hear Me Talkin' To Ya*. USA, Rinehart & Co; London, Peter Davies Ltd.

Shapiro, Nat and Hentoff, Nat: *The Jazz Makers*. London, Peter Davies Ltd.

In addition I have used a number of record reviews etc. which appeared in *Down Beat* magazine, an article in the September 11, 1975 issue of the same magazine, *Count Basie, A Hard Look at an Old Softie*, by John McDonough, and *Twenty Years With Basie* by Bill Coss in the 1957 Metronome Year Book. An interview of Basie by Charles Fox in the mid-1970s broadcast by the BBC was also extremely useful. Finally I am indebted to Frank Driggs for his essay 'Kansas City and The Southwest' which appeared in the book *Jazz* edited by Nat Hentoff and Albert J. McCarthy (New York, Rinehart; London, Cassell).